PRAISE FOR *Lifted by Angels*

"Joel J. Miller presents us with a vision of angels firmly grounded in salvation history: active at the creation of the world, involved in its fall, ministers in its salvation, servants to the Lord Jesus, harbingers of the age to come. He succeeds brilliantly in rescuing angels from the distorting effects of popular culture and revealing them to be 'more exciting, more humbling, more inspiring, and ultimately more real' than we ever imagined."

—Metropolitan Savas (Zembillas) of Pittsburgh

"In *Lifted by Angels* Joel Miller examines traditional Jewish and Christian angelology in rich and extensive detail. Especially valuable and inspiring are the author's numerous citations of beautiful patristic texts. No one will think of angels in the same way after reading this book. It is highly recommended and without reservation."

—Patrick Henry Reardon, author of *Christ in the Psalms*

"Many Christians—made uneasy by New Age or neo-pagan angel enthusiasm—are reluctant to believe in angelic interventions at all. *Lifted by Angels* restores to us our own biblical and historical understanding: that angels are God's servants and messengers."

—Frederica Mathewes-Green, author of *The Jesus Prayer*

"Angels are an important part of the Bible and of Jewish and Christian traditions, yet we have virtually ignored them. We have abandoned the angels to horror flicks and saccharine television shows. That stops here. Joel Miller's book is a necessary act of recovery."

—Jeremy Lott, editor, *RealClearReligion*

"A beautifully written study on the unique relationship between people and angels. I found it fascinating, challenging, and inspiring. Highly recommended."

—Sheila Walsh, author of *God Loves Broken People*

"We are mostly unaware of angels' presence in our midst and their influence on our lives. What a shame! Thank God for Joel J. Miller's *Lifted by Angels*, a reminder of the role that our 'cousins' play in guiding us and of their exalted place in creation."

—Brad Miner, senior editor, *The Catholic Thing*;
senior fellow, Faith & Reason Institute

"Wonderfully done and provides insight into an oft-misunderstood subject."

—Fr. Stephen Rogers, senior priest, St. Ignatius
Orthodox Church, Franklin, Tennessee

"There is an unseen spiritual world with which we humans have to deal, and Joel Miller is a fascinating and skilled guide into this invisible reality. *Lifted by Angels* will elevate your understanding of angels and their practical role in Christian spirituality."

—Todd D. Hunter, Anglican bishop; past president,
Vineyard Churches USA; author of *Our Favorite Sins*

"If we sometimes feel alone in our spiritual struggles, it might be because we have lost touch of what Christians of old knew about the unseen angels of God. In *Lifted by Angels* Miller uses Scripture, Christian art, early church writings and tradition to lift the veil between the earthly and the spiritual realms. He lifts it ever so slightly, not in speculation, but just enough for us to catch a memorable glimpse of those heavenly hosts whom God has sent to comfort and aid us on our journey home."

—James M. Kushiner, executive editor, *Touchstone:
A Journal of Mere Christianity*

LIFTED
BY
ANGELS

LIFTED
BY
ANGELS

·

The Presence and Power
of Our Heavenly Guides
and Guardians

Joel J. Miller

Thomas Nelson
Since 1798

NASHVILLE   DALLAS   MEXICO CITY   RIO DE JANEIRO

Published in Nashville, Tennessee, by Thomas Nelson. Thomas Nelson is a registered trademark of Thomas Nelson, Inc.

Thomas Nelson, Inc., titles may be purchased in bulk for educational, business, fund-raising, or sales promotional use. For information, please e-mail SpecialMarkets@ThomasNelson.com.

Unless otherwise noted, all Scripture quotations are taken from the *Revised Standard Version Catholic Edition*, © 1965 and 1966 by Division of Christian Education of the National Council of the Churches of Christ in the United States of America and published by Oxford University Press. Those marked NKJV are taken from the *New King James Version*, © 1982 by Thomas Nelson Inc. Those marked NETS are from the *New English Translation of the Septuagint*, © 2007 by the International Organization for Septuagint and Cognate Studies Inc. and published by Oxford University Press. The lone quote marked HTM is from *The Psalter According to the Seventy*, © 1974 by Holy Transfiguration Monastery.

Frontispiece: Angels from a sixteenth-century wall mural, Sucevita Monastery, Romania. All images are in the public domain and taken from Wikimedia Commons, including those on pages 20 and 117, which are made available by the Yorck Project.

Library of Congress Cataloging-in-Publication Data

Miller, Joel, 1975–
  Lifted by angels : the presence and power of our heavenly guides and guardians / Joel J. Miller.
     p. cm.
  Includes bibliographical references and index.
  ISBN 978-1-4002-0422-9
  1. Angels—Christianity. I. Title.
  BT966.3.M55 2012
  235'.3—dc23

                                                                    2012012931

Printed in the United States of America

12 13 14 15 16 QG 6 5 4 3 2 1

For my children and the
angels who watch over them

Contents

I hope to demonstrate, if I can, that there is no absurdity or incongruity in asserting a fellowship between men and angels.

AUGUSTINE, *City of God*

Author's Note

Since my aim here is to present angels as understood by the early Christians, I refer to some writings commonly collected under the name Apocrypha. Many in the ancient church counted these books—such as Tobit and the Wisdom of Solomon—as Scripture and therefore useful and edifying. As they cast light on this ancient view of angels, I hope their inclusion here is equally useful and edifying.

Writing a book requires many angels of both the literal and the figurative variety. I owe thanks to several who have offered insight, prayers, books, counsel, and more: my dear wife, Megan; my parents, Dennis and Karen; my in-laws, Mike and Gail; my godfather, Tom; the guys of the Singleton discussion group; my editors, Heather and Dimples; and also Frs. Bob, Stephen, and Pat.

Our Larger City

The Origin and Nature of the Angels

You know not altogether what angels are.
AUGUSTINE, *Expositions on the Psalms*

1

Say the word *angel* and people conjure many diff-erent images. Some picture ethereal-winged creatures in long, gossamer gowns, girlish and glowing. Others see squat, chubby cherubs with toy bows and arrows, childish and cloying. Movies and television offer us otherworldly beings here to lend a helping hand, while pop music and our grandmothers dilute the word to a simple term of endearment.

I want to paint you a different picture, one using the pigments provided by the Scripture, art, services, hymns, and teachings of the ancient Christian church. The image that forms from these sources is, I think, more exciting, more frightening, more humbling, more inspiring, and ultimately more real than our popular conceptions.[1]

This *realness* strikes me as important. Plenty of people do not believe in angels. That's nothing new. The Sadducees of Jesus' day denied their existence too.[2] But the Christian faith has always assumed the active presence of angels in the life of God's people. And what if that's right? Wouldn't that affect us? Isn't that affecting us now? I think so, and I hope in these pages to show how—particularly how angels bring us *to* and *through* a saving experience of Christ.

150 BC - 70 BC   Conservative, believed only the written
1 of 3 Jewish political / religious groups law of MOSES
Essene + Pharisees were other

As it happens, I have always believed in angels. But my belief had long gone unexamined and unexplored. Angels for me were remote and two-dimensional, perhaps more like characters in a storybook than real persons. But then I encountered a passage from Augustine's *City of God*, quoted here at the start of the book, in which he suggested not merely that angels exist, but that we have a special relationship with them, that heaven and earth share a certain fellowship.[3] That began to change things for me. Here was a vision of angels three-dimensional, immediate, and personal. For the ancient Christians this was easily assumed and readily believed, and perhaps by the end of this journey it will be the same for us.

Our course is fairly simple. In the present chapter we will look at what the early saints believed about the origin and nature of the angels. What are they like? What do they do? From there chapter 2 takes a turn. More than a plot complication, the fall of Satan and his angels represents a cosmic calamity. Chapter 2 explores this disaster as well as the fall of humanity and our subsequent alienation from God. Chapter 3 covers the dramatic story of Israel and how God used angels to nurture and protect his chosen people so they could bring forth Christ, the Lord of the angels. Chapter 4 concerns his triumph over Satan along with our participation in that victory and reconnection with God.

These chapters are in a sense historical in that they follow a narrative of past events. The later chapters are more personal, describing the times and places that our lives most commonly intersect with angels in the present. Chapter 5 examines the role of guardian angels, how they shepherd and protect us, and their role in guiding us on our path to God. Chapter 6 explores worship and how angels accompany us in our prayers, praise, and participation in the sacred mysteries. Finally, chapter 7 takes us to the end of things. The ancient Christian conviction was that angels accompany us individually when we die and also accompany Christ at his second coming.

As these seven chapters unfold, I hope we glimpse the contours of a sweeping and dramatic story of redemption, a story our ancient forebears believed wholeheartedly, a story in which the angels play a crucial role. Should we expect less? After all, asks the apostle Paul about angels in the first chapter of Hebrews, "Are they not all ministering spirits, sent forth to serve, for the sake of those who are to obtain salvation?"[4]

3

Angels have been the subject of great and wild speculation from the beginning. Because they dwell in realms unseen, they seem distant and curious. Their very inaccessibility fuels our interest and wonder, which unfortunately comes at the expense of their seeming foreign and apart. They are anything but.

Augustine famously envisioned the created order split in two camps, one of light and the other of darkness, one of love and devotion to God and the other of pride and alienation from the Creator. He termed these camps "the city of God" and "the city of the world," the former serving as the title for one of his most enduring and influential books. *City of God*, written in the early fifth century, is an ambitious work, covering a vast amount of material, including the origin and destiny of the angels.

Augustine presents us a picture of immediacy and proximity. In discussing the relationship between angels and humans, he says that we should not "suppose four cities, two of angels and two of men." Rather, "[w]e may speak of two cities, or communities, one consisting of the good, angels as well as men, and the other of the evil."[5] Heaven isn't so far off. Its borders cross our very own, and we share our city with angels. No surprise then that Augustine elsewhere suggests we consider them our neighbors.[6]

It's also no surprise that Augustine insists they are part of the church.[7] For this reason, traditional Christian communities that keep liturgical calendars celebrate various feast days for the angels. They are enumerated and enrolled with us, brothers in a shared confession.[8]

So who are these neighbors of ours, these other siblings? Holy Scripture provides the first brushstrokes, but the image is one both mysterious and complicated, even from the outset. We twice encounter angels in an opening passage of Genesis. Start with the second instance, which concludes the story of the fall. After Adam and Eve ate the forbidden fruit, God cast them from the Garden of Eden and positioned an angel or pair of angels—*cherubim* is plural—with a whirling blade of fire to prevent their return.[9] That flashing sword calls to mind the psalmist's words, those about God making his "ministers a flame of fire."[10]

The Genesis account gives no description of these angels, but scholars remind us that the word *cherub* is actually a linguistic cousin of *gryphon*. Whether picturing an eagle's head and wings with a lion's body gets us close or not, the storyteller clearly has in mind creatures fierce and formidable, nothing so easily mistaken as models for greeting-card illustrations.[11]

It's a frightening close to a grim chapter, though still not so chilling as the first angelic encounter. This one is even more disturbing for its subtlety and malevolence. Here the angel comes masked by a serpent. He is a fallen angel the leader of a whole host just like him, and he tricks Eve into disobeying God and eating the forbidden fruit.[12]

So mere pages into the biblical story we are presented with a complex picture of the angels and the wider neighborhood that we share. In just one passage, the third chapter of Genesis, angels are depicted both as guards serving at the Lord's behest and as deceivers trying to foul humanity and rupture our relationship with the Creator.

But we have also come into the story midstream. To better understand our relationship with the angels, we must go farther back.

4

This larger city of ours is one older than reckoning, and its origins lay beyond the haze of a distant horizon. Some of the early writers peered into the mystery and caught a glimpse of the start of things. In their books and homilies, they provide us a glance of our own, including a look at the creation of the angels.

Gregory Nazianzen, the fourth-century theologian, poet, and archbishop of Constantinople, saw the goodness of God as the impetus for creation. The Father, Son, and Holy Spirit require only themselves in an eternal relationship of mutual love, he explained. But love naturally seeks objects, and so an uncreated God naturally creates. "Good must be poured out and go forth," said Gregory, beyond the holy Trinity itself, "to multiply the objects of its beneficence." He considered this generosity "essential to" or characteristic of "the highest goodness." Thus God "first conceived the heavenly and angelic powers. And this conception was a work fulfilled by His Word, and perfected by His Spirit."[13] And so we have the angels.

A Syrian monk who lived a few centuries later, John Damascene, echoed this explanation. He said that "in His exceeding goodness" God "wished certain things to come into existence which would enjoy his benefits and share in His goodness, [so] He brought all things out of nothing into being and created them, both what is invisible [such as the angels] and what is visible [such as ourselves]."[14]

While Gregory's and John's observations fit the character of the Creator as revealed in Scripture, it's worth noting that Scripture itself makes only oblique reference to the creation of the angels and does not overtly reveal God's motives in creating them. Surprising as it may seem, no biblical author treats the subject— or for that matter anything else about the angels—at length. Everything we know, everything we encounter here in these pages, is instead gathered from scattered insights, arranged by theologians, preachers, hymn writers, and iconographers in a mosaic, cemented by time and tradition.

Do not let this seeming inattention to angels in Scripture disconcert. The Bible was of course written for humans and deals primarily with the story of our communion with God—its loss in Adam, restoration in Christ, and realization in the church. Angels feature in our story just as we feature in theirs, but they are not wholly the same tale. Though our lives intersect, they have their own trajectories.

That does not mean we are incapable of knowing more of their story, only that we must recognize the limited and speculative nature of our knowledge. We question; we probe; we listen; we theorize. Augustine considered all of this "a useful exercise for the intellect, if the discussion be kept within proper bounds, and if we avoid the error of supposing ourselves to know what we do not know."[15] As far as he was concerned, varying interpretations and speculations were all worthy of consideration and contemplation, provided they were also edifying and hewed to the core doctrines of received Christian teaching, what is called the rule of faith.[16]

Operating accordingly, these ancient writers reached as far over the horizon as they could manage.

5

The Bible does not explicitly say when the angels were created, but the Scripture is also quiet about the arrival of water, air, and fire, as Basil the Great noted in *The Hexaemeron*, though we know that God created them as well—and that he even uses the silence of the text to prod our curiosity and investigation.[17]

For Basil, who lived in the middle years of the fourth century, the angels were created prior to the physical world, and "the mode of the creation of the heavenly powers is passed over in silence" because the biblical writer "revealed to us only the creation of the things perceptible by sense."[18]

For others, the creation of the visible and invisible worlds was simultaneous. Connecting celestial powers and stars, some tied the angelic creation to that of the sun, moon, and stars on the fourth day. Scripture lends credence to this view by frequently linking angels and stars. Revelation 19, for instance, features an angel standing in the sun, while the ninth and twelfth chapters liken both faithful and rebel angels to stars.[19] In Judges, Deborah and Barak sang about stars making war on their enemies just a few verses from an angel doing likewise.[20] And God, speaking from the whirlwind in the book of Job, called his angels "morning stars."[21]

Augustine was not a fan of this view, confessing uncertainty about angelic involvement with celestial bodies.[22] He looked instead to creation's first day. When God spoke light into existence, he created nothing that radiated light as we understand it. The sun, moon, and stars came later. Augustine suggested in a beautiful and poetic twist that this light was the sudden reflection of God's glory from the newly created angels as they contemplated their Lord. God is light, as the apostle John says in chapter 1 of his first epistle, and now in a red-hot moment there was something created capable of reflecting him. "Thus the angels," said Augustine, "illuminated by that light by which they were created, themselves became light . . . by participation in the changeless light and day, which is the Word of God, through whom they themselves and all other things were made."[23] While attending their maker, the angels glowed.

The seventh-century monk Isaac the Syrian agreed. "[T]he [angelic] natures were created," he said, "by a verbal command, and this was light."[24]

An icon of the first day that I've seen affirms this idea. It shows Christ as Creator, aloft above the deep. He extends his hand in the sign of the cross, as if to say that the very act of creation is one of blessing. "Let there be light," he declares, and above him beams what appears to be the sun, though it cannot be that, not yet. The glowing circle serves as a symbol for the angelic light; angels, having suddenly come into existence, whirl and fly within the disc. Monreale Cathedral in Sicily features a twelfth-century mosaic of this image. The scene shows angels bursting into existence at the words of Christ, while the inscription references the creation of light. *The First Day* from the Genesis Mosaic in the narthex of St. Mark's Basilica in Venice also captures this scene, though a bit differently. As Christ creates light, two spheres appear—one red, the other blue. The red indicates the uncreated light of God; the blue represents its denial or rejection. An angel stands behind the red sphere, partially red and partially blue. The image places the creation of the angels on the first day, as did Augustine, and also shows that some would reject the light, something we'll see here in chapter 2. Though the mosaic dates to the thirteenth century, its design is informed by a fifth- or sixth-century illuminated manuscript known as the Cotton Bible.[25]

Angels are, said John Damascene, "secondary lights derived from that first light which is without beginning."[26] Maybe it's one of the reasons James, the brother of Jesus and the first bishop of Jerusalem, called God "the Father of lights" in his eponymous epistle.[27]

But God was not yet done. Pleased with these, his first creatures, "He conceive[d] a second world, material and visible," said Gregory Nazianzen, "and this is a system and compound of earth and sky, and all that is in the midst of them."[28] Such is our world, and the angels were present with God as he created it. What's more, Scripture says they were exuberant and excited by the feat.[29] They have always been in this sense like our eager, older brothers.

6

At first blush the angels seem very different from us. Scripture says they are like wind and fire, winged, and in some cases many-eyed.

They are spirits. In the language of the church they are "the honorable bodiless powers of heaven." Because they lack physicality like our own, they are described as incorporeal, rational, and noetic. Gregory Nazianzen called them "nimble intelligences."[30] Basil called them the "pure, intelligent, and other-worldly powers." Sometimes the ancient writers spoke of them as fiery, as did Basil, who identified their substance as "an ethereal spirit . . . an immaterial fire."[31]

Scripture provides the same image. The psalmist spoke of angels as winds and flames. The thirteenth chapter of Judges gives us an angel ascending to heaven in the updraft of a blazing sacrifice, while the prophets Ezekiel and Daniel described an angel in the form of a man but adorned with flames and lightning and gleaming like polished metal.[32] But these are only hints and flashes. The fullness of the angelic nature is mostly unknown to us. Only God, said John Damascene, "knows the form and limitation of its essence."[33]

We do know that angels have limits like all created beings. They are not omnipresent like God. They are "circumscribed," to use John Damascene's word. Angels have boundaries, an outline of sorts, and the stories of angels in Scripture bear this out. If they are in one place, they are not in another. But being spirits, they are not bound by our physical world. They can move rapidly, and things like walls and doors and distances mean little to them.

Despite these differences, there is a correlation between them and us. The twenty-first chapter of Revelation speaks of an angel measuring the New Jerusalem in cubits, a unit of measurement based on the length of a man's forearm. Curiously, the text tells us that it is also "an angel's."[34] And repeatedly Scripture refers to angels appearing as men, looking like men, even being mistaken for men. The earliest Christian art followed suit; fourth-century biblical frescoes from the Via Latina catacomb in Rome feature angels depicted just like men.[35] The witness of Scripture and the ancient Christians was that angels are not utterly foreign and apart; there is a certain symmetry between us, a family resemblance, if we're allowed to push it that far.

But just as not all people are alike, so angels also differ among themselves. They have individual names:

Gabriel, Michael, and Raphael, for instance. They have different places and functions. While they all maintain "the dignity of angels," according to Jerome, the translator of the Vulgate, "there are various degrees of eminence among them."[36] They vary, echoed John Damascene, in "brightness and position."[37] Some possess lesser authority and rank; others, greater power and responsibility. Scripture designates some as *angels* and *archangels*, others as *cherubim* and *seraphim*, and still others as *thrones, dominions, principalities, powers,* and *authorities.*[38]

Hierarchy, divisions, and ranks clearly point to angels having their own unique society, but Scripture provides very little detail about how it all works. In the books of Zechariah and Daniel, for instance, we see angels talk to each other and even come to each other's aid, but that's about it.[39] How these different ranks relate to each other beyond that is an open question, something confessed by both Augustine and Cyril of Jerusalem.[40] As to the organization of "this supremely happy society in heaven," Augustine suggested that "those who are able [to] answer these questions" should do so, "if they can also prove their answers to be true."

7

An anonymous fifth- or sixth-century Christian thinker, writing under the pseudonym Dionysius the Areopagite, took up Augustine's challenge. He penned a book called *The Celestial Hierarchy*, in which he gathered the scriptural information and worked it over into a systematic classification.

This Pseudo-Dionysius, as he is usually called, devised three levels, or *choirs*, each containing three types of angels. The first choir of angels included seraphim, cherubim, and thrones, ranked in that order. The second choir comprised dominions, powers, and authorities, and the third, principalities, archangels, and angels. While *angel* works as a catchall for these celestial beings, in Pseudo-Dionysius's scheme it also designated the lowest rank of heavenly creatures, the one closest to people. That rank includes guardian angels, whose primary job is to keep watch over the souls and bodies of human beings.

As we contemplate angels, it's useful to consider these designations with reference to Scripture and iconography of the church. Seraphim are mentioned explicitly in only one biblical passage, the sixth chapter of Isaiah. Traditionally considered, they are some of the angels in closest proximity to God, flying directly above his heavenly throne. They are closely identified with flame and fire, and their name implies as much.[41] Scripture offers little description except that they have six wings—"with two he covered his face, and with two he covered his feet, and with two he flew," as Isaiah recorded.[42] Icons often depict seraphim with wings that sweep across their entire bodies, or show them entirely without bodies, just six crisscrossed pinions framing an angelic face.[43]

Taking cues from descriptions in Ezekiel and Revelation, iconographers usually depict cherubim with four wings, sometimes six, and occasionally with four faces: a man's, a bull's, a lion's, and an eagle's. As we saw earlier, there is some connection between cherubim and gryphons; the Eighteenth Psalm even has God mounted atop a cherub and roaring through the air on the mighty gusts of its wings.[44] Iconographers usually play it safer than that, illustrating cherubim like the seraphim as mere faces framed by a spray of wings, sometimes with numerous eyes among the feathers.[45]

Thrones are closely related to the cherubim. Scripture describes God as enthroned upon the cherubim, and the cherubim are said to move by means of many-eyed wheels. In iconic depiction, again following Ezekiel and Daniel, thrones usually resemble red-hot rings or flaming wheels with small wings.[46]

Dominions, powers, authorities, and principalities govern various aspects of God's creation, such as regions, nations, and peoples. Though their specific functions are not much described in Scripture, allusions and references are there, such as in Deuteronomy's "Song of Moses," which says that God divided humanity under the angels, and in the book of Daniel, which discusses the angelic princes—maybe call them overlords—of Israel, Persia, and Greece.[47] Early Christian writers understood these passages as indicating angelic governance over the affairs of people. In his *Miscellanies*, for instance, Clement of Alexandria, who was born around the year 150, mentioned "regiments of angels . . . distributed over the nations and cities."[48] And John Damascene said angels "are the guardians of the divisions of the earth . . . they govern all our affairs and bring us succor."[49] Iconographers rarely attempt their particular depiction, but when they do they usually imagine them as similar, if not identical, to the remaining two classes, *archangels* and *angels*.

These latter two groups of angels are those with which people have the most direct contact. As I said before, the earliest depiction of such angels seems to have been as mere men. A second- to third-century illustration of the Annunciation found in the Catacomb of Priscilla in Rome, for instance, features Gabriel standing unwinged before Mary and clad in a simple white robe.[50] Angels ascending and descending Jacob's ladder in the Via Latina catacomb also appear as mere men.[51]

This unadorned style was soon replaced with the winged imagery to which we are more accustomed. Often painted in classical Greco-Roman style, these angels are usually shown as beardless and with long, wavy hair, bound by ribbons. Depicted with serene and gentle faces, they stand tall and sometimes sport armor and weaponry, including breastplates and shields, swords and staves. On occasion they also hold small, glowing stars, an image that recalls their origin, reflecting the light of Christ to the world.

8

With so many categories and classifications, why are they all called *angels*? Inside the answer to that question is the first and most basic relation between them and us.

Angels behold God directly, as Pseudo-Dionysius explained in *The Celestial Hierarchy*. "They look on the divine likeness with a transcendent eye," he said, adding, "They have the first and most diverse participation in the divine and they, in turn, provide the first and the most diverse revelations of the divine hiddenness." They reflect the light, and in that act of revelation angels get their name, and we begin our real relationship with them. "That is why they have a preeminent right to the title of angel or messenger," he said, "since it is they who first are granted the divine enlightenment and it is they who pass on to us these revelations which are so far beyond us."[52]

The English word *angel* is from the Greek word for "messenger," as is its Hebrew equivalent, *mal'akh*. No wonder that scriptural accounts of angelic-human interaction mostly concern passing news, explaining mysteries, giving warning, or encouraging the fearful. "They are our teachers," said Isaac the Syrian, adding that our "development and illumination cannot come to pass without the divine vision received of angels."[53]

They have other functions, of course. Exercising power over fire, restraining winds, stirring waters—these are all scriptural images of angels and their ministrations.[54] God uses angels, said Athenagoras of Athens in the second century, "to exercise providence . . . over the things created and ordered by Him; so that God may have the universal and general providence of the whole, while the particular parts are provided for by the angels appointed over them."[55] But their primary task is to reflect the knowledge and glory of God upon creation and point us to the source of that knowledge and glory.

How, if they are invisible and bodiless, do they deliver their messages to people of flesh and blood? One answer is *noetically*—through our thoughts. Angels can in a sense whisper, maybe even shout, to our spirits, minds, and hearts. People talk about having certain passing impressions or moods or imaginations. Early Christians knew that some of these thoughts were in fact angelic suggestions. "The angel of righteousness is sensitive, modest, meek, and mild," according to *The Shepherd of Hermas*, an early second-century book by the Roman Hermas. "[W]hen he rises up in your heart, he immediately speaks with you about righteousness, purity, reverence, contentment, every upright deed, and every glorious virtue. When all these things rise up in your heart, realize that the angel of righteousness is with you."[56] Such impressions come

Revelation 7.1 features four angels standing at the earth's corners, holding back the winds. This illumination from Beatus of Liébana's Commentary on the Apocalypse *represents the idea with four angels at the corners of the page, winds blowing from their mouths.*

from the Holy Spirit, but the Holy Spirit often communicates his love to us through the means of angels, something we'll explore again in chapter 5.

That said, angels are not limited to noetic communication. While bodiless and invisible, angels can condescend and make their presence palpably and tangibly known. They, said Basil, become "visible, appearing to those who are worthy in the form of bodies proper to them."[57] And so in Genesis we see Abraham and Lot offering water for angelic visitors to wash their feet while also carrying on conversation—and Jacob not only talking but physically wrestling with an angel.[58]

Augustine admitted difficulty in understanding how angels can speak *inside* us intellectually and spiritually and also *to* us audibly and bodily.[59] But he never would have considered denying the fact. Scripture records too many moments when these elder brothers of ours have visibly, physically interrupted human life.

9

Banish from the mind the idea that these were typically pleasant moments. Given the mere surprise, let alone the possible gusts of wind and fire, horror and fear make for better expectations.

When the archangel Gabriel appeared to help the prophet Daniel, he stunned the man. "I was frightened and fell upon my face," said Daniel. And frequency and familiarity failed to mellow things. In another encounter, though Gabriel goes unnamed in the text, he appeared like "a man clothed in linen, whose loins were girded with gold. . . . His body was like beryl, his face like the appearance of lightning, his eyes like flaming torches, his arms and legs like the gleam of burnished bronze, and the sound of his words like the noise of a multitude."[60] Gabriel was next forced to reach down and retrieve Daniel from the floor because the prophet had, quite naturally, blacked out at the sight. It's an example of the human mind experiencing a sort of sensory—possibly suprasensory—overload. Totally overwhelmed, Daniel almost literally fell apart.[61]

Something similar happened to Isaiah during his vision. "I saw the Lord sitting upon a throne, high and lifted up," he said, "and his train filled the temple. Above him stood seraphim," the fiery, six-winged angels. Isaiah reported that the seraphim sang aloud,

> Holy, holy, holy is the LORD of hosts;
> The whole earth is full of his glory!

As each seraph sang, Isaiah trembled. Their powerful voices shook the temple, and smoke filled the room as he felt the reverberations pulse through his body. Then God spoke, and it was all over for Isaiah. "Woe is me!" he cried in despair, utterly undone by an overwhelming experience of the holy.[62]

But angelic encounters are not always frightful or meant to be. Angelic visitors are not intent upon fear; it's entirely incidental to their purpose—perhaps only inadvertent evidence of their mission, representing the all-powerful Creator. Such visitation is primarily about revelation, about knowledge and insight from God to the people he loves. What else but love could motivate them, even in the most severe of their tasks? Created by God from the overflow of his grace, they share what they receive. So when Gabriel comforted Daniel after nearly scaring him to death, he quickly softened his appearance and assured the prophet that he was "greatly beloved."[63] And the angel was even gentler with pregnant Hagar. To escape the fury of her jealous mistress, Hagar fled to the wilderness. But then, stranded and alone, she despaired. An angel came to comfort, and Hagar indicated awe or fear only *after* she received the needed consolation.[64]

Sometimes, maybe even most of the time, angelic visitation is incognito, as happened with Raphael and Tobit, a story we'll touch on later, or when the apostle Paul said that some "have entertained angels unawares."[65]

10

Truth be told, we are mostly unaware. As Augustine said when commenting on the Eighty-sixth Psalm, we "know not altogether what angels are."[66] But our ignorance is no more inevitable than it is irreversible.

First, a caution: many of these early writers seemed at times reluctant to speak too much of angels, particularly if such talk would detract from the contemplation and worship due the Lord of the angels himself, their maker and ours.

In his letter to the church at Tralles, for instance, Ignatius of Antioch, a bishop and disciple of the apostle John, skirted the issue by saying that his readers were "still infants." He claimed knowledge of "heavenly realms and the angelic regions and hierarchies of the cosmic rulers, both visible and invisible"—which both he and his teacher John had seen in person, mind you—but declined elucidation, "otherwise you may choke, not being able to swallow enough."[67]

The apostle Paul was the same way. He had a glorious vision of heaven, but never preached from it and said instead that he resolved to preach nothing but the crucified Christ.[68] If any knowledge, even knowledge of angels, diverted attention from Christ, then faithful preachers like Paul and Ignatius ducked the subject and rerouted their listeners to the Lord and his church.

But if contemplating our fellowship with angels could increase our understanding of Christ, his mission, and the believers' role in it, then further comment seems not only warranted, but perhaps even necessary. Indeed, why else would Paul and these early Christians talk of angels at all? But they do, and these savvy practitioners point the way for us today.

So picture again this larger, shared city of ours. There are countless avenues down which to venture and explore. Some passageways are better lit than others, but most illuminate aspects of our mutual experience with the angels. Taken together, they tell a fascinating story of salvation and reconciliation with God, of temptation and spiritual warfare, of community and communion, of prayer and praise. We will examine several such avenues in the coming pages.

Through it all, at every turn, at every encounter, we find over and again that the angels pierce this porous present, this fragile moment of ours that seems so solid and certain. As with our forebears, so with us: God sends his angels to live among us and lift our fallen humanity toward Christ.

Falls from Grace

The Descent of Satan, His Angels, and Us

> *Was not that Lucifer an angel once?*
> CHRISTOPHER MARLOWE, *Doctor Faustus*

1

Angels present us with every kind of good. They love; they serve; they share; they instruct; they worship. But there's another side to the angels' story, a dark chapter, and we now open those grim pages. There is light ahead, but we must first traverse the shadows.

Evil is evident in the world, and despite what some might say, this evil is something more than man's prejudices and hatreds projected on his surroundings and neighbors, something far worse than a generic, destructive principle blowing through the world like bad spiritual weather.[1] According to the ancient witnesses, evil began in a person. And it began in, of all places, heaven.

There are several visions of heaven in Scripture: Isaiah, Ezekiel, Daniel, John, and others peered through the veil and saw God upon his throne. They saw him surrounded by angels, the circling seraphim, cherubim, and others, singing thunderous, rapturous praise, choir upon choir of the heavenly host offering antiphonal adoration, their acclamation echoing and pulsing through celestial halls.

But it's a mistake to assume a full house. Heaven is a broken home. God created angels as objects of his love and beneficence, and though most rejoiced in their status, returning the affection of their Creator in ceaseless waves of gratitude, others among them did the unthinkable. They rebelled.

We began this book by talking about two cities. Here we meet the inhabitants of the second: fallen angels, demons, and evil spirits. Their ongoing mutiny is led by Satan, a once privileged angel sometimes called Lucifer. The name means "light-bearer," for so he once was. But no longer. He is now, in the memorable phrase of one second-century bishop, Irenaeus of Lyons, the "ringleader of the apostasy."[2]

2

The angels were created good, but not all stayed that way. Satan and those that joined him corrupted themselves and turned against God. As a result, we find angels "charged with error" and the heavens declared unclean in the book of Job. We similarly find the second of Peter's epistles talking about angels who sinned and Jude's short letter saying some angels "did not keep their own position but left their proper dwelling."[3]

It was not supposed to be this way. Gregory Nazianzen confessed the desire to say that angels always chose good, but he could not do it "because of him who for his splendor was called Lucifer, but became and is called Darkness through his pride; and the apostate hosts who are subject to him, creators of evil by their revolt against good."[4] Satan, as John Damascene elaborated,

> was not made wicked in nature but was good, and made for good ends, and received from his Creator no trace whatever of evil in himself. But he did not sustain the brightness and the honor which the Creator had bestowed on him, and of his free choice was changed from what was in harmony to what was at variance with his nature, and became roused against God who created him, and determined to rise in rebellion against him: and he was the first to depart from good and become evil. . . . But along with him an innumerable host of angels subject to him were torn away and followed him and shared in his fall. Wherefore . . . they became wicked, turning away at their own free choice from good to evil.[5]

What exactly happened is a difficult question. Though early Christians universally believed in the reality of the angelic fall, universal agreement about the details eluded them. "[T]he ecclesiastical teaching maintains that [evil spirits] do indeed exist," said an evidently frustrated Origen, "but what they are or how they exist is not explained with sufficient clarity."[6] The Devil unsurprisingly lurks in these details as much as in any others. To begin sorting them out, we turn to the Garden of Eden, where lurks a serpent.

3

According to the Genesis account, God created man and woman, placed them in the Garden of Eden, and gave them freedom to possess and enjoy it. Only one tree was forbidden, the taste of its fruit to remain unknown. But then a serpent came and tempted Eve to eat the fruit. She fell for his ruse. Eve rationalized the action, tasted the fruit, and gave some to Adam, who also ate. Their disobedience turned love to fear and divine communion to alienation. Suddenly conscious of their sin, the pair ran and hid, but the hiding proved futile. God discovered the sin, cursed the serpent, and sent Adam and Eve away.[7]

While Satan escapes direct mention in the story, from the beginning Christians pegged him as the silent—or at least unseen—partner in the temptation.

And not without biblical warrant. The twelfth chapter of Revelation speaks, for instance, of Satan as "that ancient serpent . . . the deceiver of the whole world."[8] Some early Christian writers like Justin Martyr identified the serpent and Satan so closely as to make them interchangeable figures.[9] Other writers allowed that they were separate but conspired together. As Irenaeus saw it, for instance, the snake "bore the Devil." Satan, he said, spoke through the serpent.[10]

An intriguing question is, why would Eve listen to a snake in the first place? We can only assume that prior to the serpent's curse it was in some sense noble and attractive, something from which Eve would not recoil. The serpent was "loved by God," according to the pseudepigraphal *The Life of Adam and Eve*, an ancient book read and used by Jews and Christians. Satan employed him because Eve would "give credence to [the serpent] before any other creature."[11] Interestingly, serpents and seraphim are linguistic neighbors; perhaps Eve's snake was more like a dazzling angel before its curse. Clearly it was an upright creature in mind and stature because the text says that the serpent was wise and only slithered on its belly as a result of the curse.[12]

And Satan's motive? The trouble began right after God suggested making people in the divine image. "God created man for incorruption, and made him in the image of his own eternity [or nature]," according to the Wisdom of Solomon, "but through the devil's envy death entered the world."[13] Envy of man, jealousy of his undeserved immortality and divine image, drove the Devil to undermine him in the Garden. But that envy first undermined the Devil himself, being the very source of his fall.

An angel drives Adam and Eve from the Garden while a cherub with eyes in his wings stands guard at the gate. From a mosaic at the Cathedral of Monreale in Palermo, Sicily.

Said Irenaeus, "[B]ecause of the many gifts of God" to man, the Devil "became jealous and looked on him with envy, and so ruined himself and made the man a sinner, persuading him to disobey the commandment of God. So, the angel becoming, by falsehood, the head and originator of sin, was himself struck, having offended God, and caused the man to be cast out of the Paradise."[14]

Cyprian of Carthage, writing in the mid-third century, saw it the same way. Even though Satan was originally majestic and loved by God, "when he beheld man made in the image of God, [Satan] broke forth into jealousy with malevolent envy—not hurling down another by the instinct of his jealousy before he himself was first hurled down by jealousy, captive before he takes captive, ruined before he ruins others."[15]

Consulting *The Life of Adam and Eve* proves useful here. As the story goes, God made Adam in his image, and the angels bowed to man as the image of God. But Satan would not bow, even when ordered to do so by the archangel Michael. Satan was created first and would not serve this latecomer. Satan's heart soured as Adam was given preeminence. Provoking the other angels over the perceived outrage, the Devil led some of them away into rebellion. But Satan was not satisfied with the wreckage he had made of his life and the lives of his fallen followers. He decided next to unseat man, to spoil God's creation. To accomplish his ends he chose an ally: the serpent. Satan stirred resentment in his heart, telling him that bowing to the latecomer was unfitting, unfair, and intolerable. He was, after all, also created before man. The serpent bought the lie and defected, allowing the Devil to speak lies to Eve through him, providing his glory to mask the envious intentions of the vile angel.[16]

4

Looking at the story of Eden, Augustine said that the Devil "administered to man that cup of pride by which [he] was cast down. For this fallen [angel] said to man, envying his standing, 'Taste, and you shall be as gods;' that is, seize to yourselves by usurpation that which you are not made, for I also have been cast down by robbery."[17]

Note the mention of pride. In Paul's first letter to Timothy, he seems to indicate that pride caused the Devil's fall.[18] As Augustine understood it, pride is the source of all sin, and envy flows from it like a fetid stream. Pride elevates the self, while envy then turns to bring others down. But this may be too fine a distinction. Pride and envy are related and even simultaneous impulses—both characterized by ingratitude.[19]

On that point, notice Augustine's image of the cup, which calls to mind the Eucharist, the act of offering thanks and gratitude to God through the chalice on behalf of all creation. Satan's sin began by refusing to offer thanks and grace. God made all things through an overflow of his goodness, but Satan rejected that goodness. He would instead take what he considered his own by robbery. He would not receive. Instead he would take.

How this corruption operates in the heart is helpful to understand. Fourth-century bishop Gregory of Nyssa, a close friend of Gregory Nazianzen and the younger brother of Basil the Great, explained it at length in section 6 of his *Great Catechism*. Satan, he said, "closed his eyes to the good and the ungrudging like one who in the sunshine lets his eyelids down upon his eyes and sees only darkness." By shutting out the good, he "became [aware] of the contrary to goodness." When one contemplates goodness, thankfulness and gratitude arise. But to spurn it is to nurture ingratitude, which sprouts a host of corrupting thoughts and emotions, particularly envy.[20]

Gregory's image of closed eyes takes on added significance when recalling that angels were illumined by the knowledge of God as they contemplated their Creator. To close the eyes was for Satan to separate himself from the knowledge of God, to cut himself off from the experience of his maker, to turn his back on his benefactor. And that's exactly what he did.

As Satan nurtured envy in his heart, he set in motion the utter corruption of his being. Gregory compared his fall to that of a rock from a mountain face: "[H]e, dragged away from his original natural propensi[ty] to goodness and gravitating with all his weight in the direction of vice, was deliberately forced and borne away as by a kind of gravitation to the utmost limit of iniquity."[21]

Having rejected goodness, Satan turned all his energies against what was good. He made his "better endowments . . . instrument in the discovery of contrivances for the purposes of vice, while by his crafty skill he deceives and circumvents man, persuading him to become his own murderer with his own hands." The newly created image of God was given preeminence, appointed by God as "king over the earth and all things on it," as Gregory said. Man and woman were regal, beautiful. They enjoyed an intimate relationship with their Creator. All of this, said Gregory, fueled Satan's "passion of envy."[22]

Ingratitude begets envy. Satan was corrupted by it and then used it to corrupt the other fallen angels and the serpent, who in turn encouraged the same sin in Eve. *God is holding out on you*, he said in so many words. *You deserve better. You deserve more.* But not so.

God provides the ultimate picture of other-focused love, always pouring out himself in and through the Trinity, in and through his creation. Satan provides the opposite image: first holding back—unwilling to give, to grant, to love—and then striking out to hurt, to maim, and to destroy.

5

There is of course a twist in the story. As I said at the outset, the ancient Christian teaching on Satan differs among the teachers. All identify envy or pride as the primary motive for Satan's fall, but they vary on the object of the envy, the point of the pride, and the order of events.

For those like Irenaeus, Cyprian, and Gregory of Nyssa, Satan became envious of humanity and fell following our creation. But others suggested that Satan first envied God and fell at some point prior to human creation. Jealous of the Creator's glory, Satan wanted it for his own. But his ambitions failed him. "[H]e who wished to make himself equal with God, while he was not so, fell, and . . . became a devil," said Augustine.[23] This later view differs from the view we've already discussed and eventually eclipsed it. Augustine's contemporary, the Scythian monk John Cassian, claimed that it was the accepted view by their day.[24] It's also the reason that the name *Lucifer* slipped into common use.

Why the change? It goes back to a certain approach to Scripture. Finding new interpretations of the Hebrew Scriptures is common enough in these early writings. Unsurprisingly, Christians saw things in Jewish texts that Jews did not. Christ himself did this and regularly explained things in Scripture that his followers and his detractors had never before seen. Satan received the same exegetical treatment, particularly as it involved the idea of pride that seeks equality with God.

Reading the judgments against the kings of Tyre and Babylon in the Prophets, some Christian teachers saw veiled references to Satan's fall. According to Ezekiel, Eden's "anointed cherub" made his "heart [like] the heart of a god" and "corrupted [his] wisdom for the sake of [his] splendor." So God "cast [him] as a profane thing out of the mountain of God."[25] In Isaiah, the self-vaunting figure claims to "ascend . . . above the stars of God" and make himself "like the Most High" but is "brought down to Sheol, to the depths of the Pit."[26] The name *Lucifer* and its identification with Satan come from this interpretation of Isaiah. Tertullian and Origen seem its earliest proponents, but the view gained wide and rapid acceptance, perhaps through the influence of Gregory Nazianzen and then Jerome, both of whom esteemed Origen.[27]

This view clearly differs from its predecessor. Less participant and more observer after the fact, humanity really doesn't have a role in this story. Satan fell because he envied God, not us. But while acknowledging the differences, it's worth noting that these two views are not mutually exclusive, not strictly, and might even be mutually reinforcing.

Prudentius, a fourth-century Spanish poet, successfully harmonized the two story lines. In his epic poem, *The Origin of Sin*, Prudentius at first seemed to follow the later view, speaking of "a being of most beauteous features," who "grew overweening in his greatness; puffed with the excessive strength to which he had grown, bearing himself too highly in his big-swelling pride, and displaying his fires more boastfully than was proper." He said that this figure became "corrupt of his own will because envy marked him with her stain and pricked him with her sore stings." Why? Prudentius, having borrowed from the later view, now takes up the earlier understanding: "He had seen how a figure fashioned of clay grew warm under the breath of God and was made lord of the creation."[28]

Prudentius wasn't alone. As the new view took root, Christians went back and edited *The Life of Adam and Eve* and similar stories then circulating, modifying them with direct quotes and allusions from these reimagined prophetic passages. The Latin version of *The Life of Adam and Eve*, for instance, takes the words from Isaiah—"I will place my seat above the stars of heaven and I will be like the Most High"—and puts them on Satan's lips as words about himself.[29] Because transmitting the core of the tradition does not hang upon rigid history, it is easy to see how more imaginative versions of the story mixed and matched differing details without diluting the essential character of the teaching—that envy corrupts and pride goes before a fall.

It's difficult to reconcile these differences, but it's not really necessary to do so. Agreeing on the precise moment that Satan and the angels fell—either before or after the creation of man—is less important than recognizing that their fall actually happened and resulted in our own corruption through Adam and Eve.[30]

6

The *fall* of humanity was more figurative than literal. But we're invited to see the angelic descent more literally. The second letter of Peter, for instance, says, "God did not spare the angels who sinned, but cast them down."[31] We get the picture of plummeting, flailing figures.

Two passages sometimes come into play here, the tenth chapter of Luke and the twelfth of Revelation. In the first, Jesus said that he saw "Satan fall like lightning from heaven."[32] The second deals with a scene of heavenly war after which Satan and a third of the angels are cast down.[33] We will explore these two passages in chapter 4, where I hope to draw out their meaning more fully. For now, we note that the fallen angels are no longer in heaven, but prowl this atmosphere of ours.

The ancients imagined a world divided into strata, moving downward from heaven to earth in layers at first refined and ethereal and then coarse and firm. In this scheme, the air is the span between the moon and the earth, the region Paul mentioned in Ephesians when he referred to Satan as "the prince of the power of the air."[34]

The atmosphere is the haunt of demons. Said John

Chrysostom in his *Homilies on Ephesians*, "Satan occupies the space under Heaven, and . . . the incorporeal powers are spirits of the air, under his operation."[35] His demons, said Prudentius, "bear rule over the damp and heavy-clouded air."[36] And said John Cassian, capturing the horror of the unheavenly host, "[T]he atmosphere which extends between heaven and earth is ever filled with a thick crowd of spirits, which do not fly about in it quietly or idly, so that most fortunately the divine providence has withdrawn them from human sight."[37]

Cassian said "fortunately" because these fallen angels are terrible to behold, changing as they do through the shapes and forms of innumerable grotesqueries while committing endless acts of depravity, wickedness, and crime. If God did not shield people's eyes, said Cassian, "men would either be driven out of their wits by an insufferable dread and faint away from inability to look on such things with bodily eyes, or else would daily grow worse and worse, and be corrupted by their constant example and by imitating them, and thus there would arise a sort of dangerous familiarity and deadly intercourse between men and the unclean powers of the air."[38]

Ever since Milton's *Paradise Lost*, people employ the word *pandemonium* to mean utter chaos, but we know that the demons retain some form of order, some form of society. The archangel Gabriel informed Daniel about dealing with the demon princes over Persia and Greece, and the apostle Paul refers to dark principalities and powers.[39] We imagine the angelic choirs twisted into demonic organizations and structures of control.

The picture is one of hierarchy and levels of power, differing ranks and duties. But unlike heaven's, hell's hierarchy is without humility. Beings motivated by envy and pride are incapable of self-debasement and service. They are only capable of self-vaunting and coercion, and evil is their only occupation.

Thoroughly corrupt, Satan and his host desire only evil continually. There is not a moment, said Cassian, in which they "desist from their wickedness." They have no need of rest, no need for food; there is nothing to slow them down. Nothing "forces them . . . to desist from the purposes they have begun to carry out."[40]

7

Though invisible, demons have not escaped Christian iconographers. Instead of robust figures with strong arms and regal bearing, fallen angels are usually depicted as spindly, scant figures with scrawny wings. Perhaps more significant, they're depicted as shadowy bluish or blackened creatures, indicating their separation from the light in which they were created. The first-century *Epistle of Barnabas* refers to Satan as the "Black One" to describe this reality,[41] and as we saw earlier, Gregory Nazianzen employed the name "Darkness" for the same purpose.

For the demons this darkness is permanent. Though humanity fell in Adam and Eve, we have the possibility of repentance, of being rejoined in communion with God. Not so for demons. "[T]he Creator of all good has imparted no grace for the reparation of angelic evils," said Augustine.[42]

God grants the grace of repentance as an allowance for our physicality and the weakness inherent to it, according to John Damascene. Eve fell because she succumbed to temptation. Adam's failure is not identified, but moral weakness is clear. We are likewise swayed by our senses, prone to fall in our passions, weariness, and so on. But angels do not have weak bodies. They behold God consciously and constantly. So while man "comes to have repentance" because of "the weakness of his body," said John Damascene, the angelic nature "is not [capable] of repentance because it is incorporeal."[43]

As recipients of God's great goodness, the fallen angels were capable of expressing the goodness they received, but because of their envy, said Augustine, "they became all the more detestably ungrateful for his beneficence."[44]

8

Corrupted by envy, the demons now turn it upon us. Unable—and unwilling—to have restoration of their own, they work feverishly to prevent ours. Having deceived our parents in the Garden, they wrap delusion around our eyes to block the angelic light.

Satan, who knows his fate, now endeavors "to make his situation our own," according to the fifth-century ascetic known as Mark the Monk. He imagined Satan's train of thought: "Just as they have become my partners in evil, so too shall they be my companions in punishment.... Just as [God] cast human beings out of paradise because of their one transgression and handed them over to death, so too shall he condemn them to be punished eternally with me for the additional evils they do."[45]

Thus Adam and Eve woke the day after the fall as residents in the city of the world, neighbors of demons intent upon their permanent residency. And here begins the central human drama. Having followed the counsel of "his cruel enemy," as Prudentius said, man now "stands between the Lord of life and the teacher of death. On the one hand God calls him, on the other the devil, the while he [man] wavers and goes from side to side."[46] The question is, whom will we serve, God or Satan?

It's a simple question with a difficult answer, and God seems at a curious and unlikely disadvantage. He granted people the choice, but the difficulty lies primarily in our choosing to serve the Lord. As Gregory of Nyssa characterized Satan's declination, the pull of sin similarly draws humanity away from God and down toward the widening maw of our primordial foe. God must reach down and pull us up.

But how? After the fall, humanity wanted little to do with our maker. But God, whose very character is love, chose to work with us nonetheless. He would coax and lead. He would chasten and encourage, pull and prod. He would shout, and he would whisper. And he would send angels to nudge and draw and urge us on the way back home to the city of God.

3

Celestial Stewards

Angels and Their Watchful Care of Israel

And we in wardship to thine angels be.
JOHN DONNE, "THE LITANY"

1

God graced Adam and Eve with kingship over the earth, but our parents disobeyed and dropped their crowns. "You were appointed ruler of creation," said Basil the Great, "and you have renounced the nobility of your own nature." Worse, we made ourselves "prisoner[s] of the devil" by the abdication, while Satan clambered into our empty throne.[1] That's the human condition east of Eden. Humanity surrendered itself to the Devil.[2]

With humanity under his thumb, Satan assumed power over the earth. *Ruler of the age, prince of the power of the air, god of this world*—these are all names and titles used by Jesus, Paul, and others about the Devil and his reign.[3] "The Evil One," said Ephraim the Syrian, "[wove] a crown of lies—and set up his throne, as god in the world."[4] He "possessed the world," said Cyril of Alexandria, "all was subject to him, and there was no man able to escape the meshes of his overwhelming might: he was worshipped by every one: everywhere he had temples and altars for sacrifice, and an innumerable multitude of worshippers."[5]

The mind turns on at least two points here. First, the Devil desires to be like God and acts as if he is. But having rejected goodness, he can only oppress and enslave. Second, rather than pour out his grace on others, he seeks theirs for himself. He craves worship. And so, said Irenaeus, he "deceive[d] and [led] astray the mind of man into disobeying the commandments of God, and gradually [darkened] the hearts of those who would endeavor to serve him, to the forgetting of the true God, but to the adoration of himself as God."[6]

Thankfully our subjection is not permanent. Despite our betrayal, God moved to rescue us from the peril into which we plunged ourselves. And he sent his angels to aid in the mission. "The single Providence of the Most High for all commanded the angels to bring all peoples to salvation," said Pseudo-Dionysius. As it happened in history, only one nation at first responded. By and large, he said, "it was Israel alone which returned to the Light and proclaimed the true Lord."[7]

To ensure that his plan would reach fruition, God nurtured and sheltered Israel in a cold and hostile world—one where demons held sway and the great mass of people lived in delusion, worshipping false gods. And so the Lord charged angels with the care of his chosen people. Their story starts with Abraham.

2

While Abraham lived in the land of Haran, situated in present-day Turkey, God spoke and told him to leave his father's house and settle in a new place. The Lord promised to bless him and bless the entire world through his descendants. So Abraham obeyed, upped stakes, and moved south to Canaan.[8]

Once Abraham was settled, God further unfolded the plan and promised a special heir. Three angels came to visit him by the oak of Mamre. They appeared as men, but Abraham, who had conversed with God, somehow recognized them as an appearance of his divine acquaintance. One of the three prophesied that Abraham and his wife, Sarah, despite their old age, would give birth to a son.[9]

Abraham and his three visitors, taken from a mosaic at the Cathedral of Monreale in Palermo, Sicily.

The angels had other work as well. Abraham's nephew, Lot, lived in the nearby city of Sodom, a place whose inhabitants had fully succumbed to demonic influence. As reports of the city's evil filled God's ears, he sent angels to investigate. After first visiting with Abraham, they turned to visit Sodom, though one stayed behind to haggle with Abraham for the lives of the righteous in the city. There were none. Faced with the people's extreme wickedness, the angels blinded an angry mob to protect Lot's family before escorting them out of town. Next the angels returned and destroyed the city.[10]

The unsettling message is clear, one that reverberates through the subsequent millennia: death is the only outcome for those who side with the Devil and live in persistent evil and delusion. The opposite is also true: those who follow the voice of God and partake of his divine life are granted life.[11]

Soon Abraham's promised child arrived. He named him Isaac. While the name means "laughter," one event early in his life occasioned much more solemnity than gladness. In a test of Abraham's trust and obedience, the Lord told him to sacrifice the young boy. Abraham agreed to do so, but having shown unfeigned loyalty to God, he was stopped from completing the deed. An angel intervened at the last moment and then reiterated the previous promises of blessing.[12]

Isaac grew, and sometime later Abraham sent his steward, Eliezer, to fetch a wife for his son. "The LORD," said Abraham, "will send his angel with you and prosper your way."[13] The angel looked out for Isaac once before and did so again, leading Eliezer to the young woman Rebekah. In time the pair had two sons, Esau and Jacob, the latter of whom also had an intense experience with God's angels.

3

Jacob's story starts badly enough.

After some tricky dealings with his father and a

murderous threat from his elder twin, Esau, Jacob fled for safer parts. Night fell, and the weary fugitive laid down his head. He dreamt of angels traversing a ladder spanning heaven and earth. Despite Jacob's shifty dealings, God did love him and intended to fulfill his pledge to Abraham through him and his children. The Lord promised to stay close to Jacob, to bring him home again, and—echoing the promise made to Abraham—to bless all the peoples of the world through his offspring.[14]

"God clearly showed what great care He took toward Jacob," commented Ephraim the Syrian, "that he was being watched not only when he was awake, but even in his sleep there were angels who were commanded to ascend and descend around him to protect him."[15]

Jacob's angelic experiences intensified over his life. The angels in his dream went quietly about their business, ascending and descending. But later, after several years away, an angel gave him audible instructions in a dream, telling him to make his way back home.[16] And then the dreams became tangible. While heading back to his father's land and fearing an armed face-off with his brother, Jacob encountered an entire troop of angels. "[T]he angels of God met him," as Genesis says, "and when Jacob saw them he said, 'This is God's army!'"[17] Esau may have had scads of men and weaponry, but Jacob had a squad of angels ready to protect him.

"Just as God had shown Jacob the angels that

accompanied him when he went down," commented Ephraim, "He also showed him angels when he was going up . . . so that he would not fear Esau."[18]

As it happened, Esau's rage had cooled in the years since Jacob's hasty departure. Esau desired only reconciliation, though Jacob had a fight on his hands nonetheless. Before meeting his brother, he encountered an angel and then wrestled with him. Genesis says only that Jacob wrestled a man, but the prophet Hosea later identified the opponent as an angel, adding that Jacob won the match.[19] The reason for the fight is not given, but imagining the angel as a celestial steward provides a hint. It was not a life-or-death fight. It was a training bout. It was testing.

It seemed an even match. Neither one held an advantage for long, and the pair fought until dawn. "He both overcame the angel and was overcome," said Ephraim, "so that [Jacob] learned both how weak he was and how strong he was. He was weak when the angel touched the hollow of his thigh and it became dislocated, but he was strong, for the angel said to him, 'Let me go.'"[20]

God used the angelic encounter to develop Jacob's faith and further establish his redemptive plan through Jacob's descendants. The angel wounded him but then blessed him when Jacob refused to let go, giving him the name *Israel*, which implied by etymology that the struggle was divine, a wrestling match with God himself somehow mediated by—experienced through—the presence of the angel. Jacob and his children would be known by the name ever after.

At the end of his life, Jacob credited the angel for preserving him to that hour, speaking of "the angel who has redeemed me from all evil," one of the earliest statements indicating belief in personal or guardian angels.[21]

4

While Jacob was still alive, he and his family migrated south to Egypt to avoid the effects of a terrible famine. But over time, the people became enslaved. For several hundred years the Israelites grew in population and became a substantial people, but they were a slave nation within a nation of oppressors—a picture of all humanity under the dominion of Satan. From this subjugated people, God called Moses to deliver Israel.

Moses first encountered God in the wilderness through an angelic presence in a flaming bush that, while engulfed by fire, was not consumed by the flames. God spoke through the angel and gave Moses directions and a plan. Moses responded in obedience and then led the people to freedom. The angel then manifested before the traveling Israelites in a pillar of cloud by day and a pillar of fire by night, at one point protecting the people as they crossed the Red Sea by blocking the advance of the pursuing Egyptian army.[22]

With Egypt now behind him, Moses met again with the angel on Mount Sinai to receive God's commandments for his people. Perhaps we imagine men like Abraham, Jacob, and Moses conversing directly with God. But whether at Mamre's oak or at the foot of the burning bush, Scripture suggests—and most ancient Christian writers affirmed—that the conversations took place through angels. The Lord's words and appearances were, in Augustine's phrase, "wrought by angels," words that only rephrase those of the martyr Stephen and the apostle Paul.[23]

Such visions are called *theophanies*, divine appearances. "The recipients of such visions," said Pseudo-Dionysius, "are granted divine enlightenment and are somehow initiated in the divine things themselves. Yet it was the heavenly powers [the angels] which initiated our venerable ancestors to these divine visions."[24]

Such an understanding stands opposite any view that sees God as distant, aloof, or uninvolved. When the angel of the Lord appeared to Gideon, for instance, he told Gideon that God was with him. Gideon objected. If that was so, he said, why were his people under oppression? Notice this: "The LORD turned to him and said, 'Go . . . and deliver Israel from the hand of [the oppressors]; do not I send you?'"[25] The *angel of the Lord* first appeared, but the *Lord* himself turned. Over and again, the Scripture shifts the participants' identity in these angelic/divine encounters. It's a literary device inviting us to contemplate that both are true, both are happening. The presence of the angel indicates the presence of God.

Iconography presents this understanding as well. As Moses unties his sandals before the burning angel, for example, a common depiction of the event reveals the hand of God reaching down from heaven. So we see the angel and the Lord in simultaneous, unified communication. Versions of this depiction are many, including a sixth-century mosaic in the Basilica of San Vitale in Ravenna, Italy, and even a third-century wall painting in the Dura-Europos synagogue in Syria, indicating an understanding shared by Christians and Jews.[26]

5

More than give the Law, the Lord granted Israel a custodian and protector. "Behold," said God, "I send an angel before you, to guard you on the way and to bring you to the place which I have prepared." Who is this angel? Although the angel is unnamed in this text, the book of Daniel later identifies Israel's angelic prince as the archangel Michael. God continued, "Give heed to him and hearken to his voice, do not rebel against him, for he will not pardon your transgression; for my name is in him. But if you hearken attentively to his voice and do all that I say, then I will be an enemy to your enemies and an adversary to your adversaries."[27]

One example comes through the account of Balaam and his loquacious donkey. Succumbing to greed and the promise of easy lucre, the seer Balaam went to serve a local king who wanted him to curse Israel. As he journeyed, an angel stood astride the road with a drawn sword. Ironically, the *seer* couldn't *see* the angel. Luckily his donkey did and swerved from the path. But blind Balaam drove her back onto the road. Again the donkey tried to avert the angel, so Balaam struck her and drove her forward. When the poor beast finally just sat down beneath him, Balaam really went to work. Suddenly, astonishingly, amid the blows the donkey blurted her verbal disapproval, introducing an amusing exchange that culminated in Balaam's eyes opening. And then he could see what stood only steps away. The angel, sword at the ready, said that Balaam owed his very life to his stubborn donkey and commanded the prophet to then see the king but to speak only words that the angel would provide. Hired to curse Israel, Balaam followed the lead of the angel and instead offered a string of blessings.[28]

Along with protection, God offered provision. As the Israelites wandered through the desert, there was insufficient forage and no time to plant and harvest. So God sent manna from heaven, called poetically (and mystically as we will see later) the "bread of the angels."[29] Despite all that God gave, however, Israel had a penchant for waywardness, and God prolonged their time in the wilderness to discipline them.

Following Moses' death, the time came to enter the promised land. It fell to Moses' captain, Joshua, to lead the people. The angel came to Joshua to encourage him before the invasion of Canaan, but despite his leadership the Israelites eventually failed in their mission. When God first promised his angel, he cautioned his people about worshipping false gods. This would mean succumbing to the same demonic delusion that enslaved the surrounding peoples. These gods would ensnare them, he warned. But they disregarded the warning. Instead of destroying the idols they encountered, the Israelites sometimes—oftentimes—worshipped the old gods and fell into immorality.[30]

The Lord's angel tolerated Israel's waywardness for many years but eventually grew weary. Confronting the people, the angel reminded them of God's warning and how their disobedience meant enslavement to false gods.[31] The prophecy came true. In Canaan, the promised land, the Israelites nurtured ingratitude like Satan himself, turning to worship demons instead of the Lord who delivered them.[32] And so, said Prudentius, humanity "scorn[ed] the author of his life, [did] homage to his own destruction, worship[ped] the bloody assassin, [and paid] reverence to the edge of the sword that [was] to murder him."[33]

The situation was precarious—and exactly what Satan desired. Here, perched on the edge of a razor, stood the hope of the nations, the people through whom all peoples would be blessed. But though Israel was ready to fall, all was not lost.

God commissioned faithful judges and prophets to call back his people, and angels sped to strengthen and protect them in their task. Accordingly we find the birth of Samson being foretold by an angel, Gideon taking encouragement and direction from an angel, and Isaiah's lips being purged by a seraph with a burning coal from the heavenly altar before receiving his divine commission.[34]

6

As it turned out, Israel's greatest enemies were its own leaders, corrupt rulers who heeded the serpent's call and dragged the nation into further idolatry.

After a successful showdown with the priests of the false god Baal, the prophet Elijah was forced to flee the wrath of the tyrannical queen Jezebel. Having escaped several miles into the wilderness, he stopped to rest. Dejected and demoralized, Elijah wanted to die for all the grief and failure he faced. He curled up under a tree and fell asleep, hoping to perish in the night.

But then an angel came. "[B]ehold, an angel touched him," says the account, and the reader can immediately sense the apparent tenderness and concern, like a soft, warm light enveloping the prophet. The angel brought bread and water to Elijah, who roused and ate before drifting back to sleep. After Elijah had rested further, the angel woke him again with a touch and fed him, and this time Elijah felt restored.[35]

In one of his last prophetic acts before his famous whirlwind exit, Elijah condemned King Ahaziah for his idolatry. Wounded after a fall, the king asked his servants to solicit his prognosis from the priests of Baalzebub, a local pagan god, whose name later became synonymous with Satan, the prince of demons.[36] An angel came to Elijah and instructed him to intercept the servants and give them a message for the king. "Is it because there is no God in Israel," the angel instructed Elijah to say, "that you are going to inquire of Baalzebub, the god of Ekron? Now therefore thus says the LORD, 'You shall not come down from the bed to which you have gone, but you shall surely die.'"[37]

Telling the servants was one thing, but Elijah next had to tell the king to his face. He froze. But the angel was there with an encouraging word and told him not to worry. So, guarded by his angel, Elijah visited the king and pronounced the judgment, after which the corrupt ruler died.[38]

As one might imagine, this was risky business. But the prophets could count on angelic protection until God's work for them was done. After all, the psalmist declared that God's angel "encamps around those who fear him, and delivers them."[39] And also:

You will not be afraid of nocturnal fright,
    of an arrow that flies by day,
of a deed that travels in darkness,
    of mishap and noonday demon. . . .
No evil shall come before you,
    and no scourge shall come near your covert,
because he will command his angels concerning you
    to guard you in all your ways;
upon hands they will bear you up
    so that you will not dash your foot against a stone.[40]

Angelic protection accompanied faithfulness. But turning one's back on God and serving the Devil meant that protection was removed—not just for the individual, but also for the whole nation.

Soon enough, foreign powers descended upon God's unfaithful people, though protection remained for those who held fast. Take the story of Elijah's replacement, Elisha. When the Syrian army warred against Israel, the Syrian king wanted Elisha eliminated because the prophet repeatedly spoiled the invaders' plans. So he sent a large detachment to surround and capture the prophet. They came in the night, and by morning the entire city where Elisha stayed was surrounded.

When Elisha's servant saw the host, he melted with fear. "Alas, my master!" said the servant. "What shall we do?" Elisha seemed oddly untroubled. He prayed that the servant could see what he already did: recalling Jacob's revelation of the angelic camp, a celestial army of fiery horses and chariots surrounded the Syrians. Elisha and his servant had nothing to fear.[41]

7

As we explore how angels upheld God's people, it's useful to note that angelic protection went beyond mere physical defense. Sometimes celestial assistance assumed an almost legal, courtroom quality. Demons thrive on accusations. In the twelfth chapter of Revelation, for instance, Satan is called the "accuser of our brethren." It says that he stood before God and "accuse[d] them day and night."[42]

Job serves as the prime example. Though Job loved God, Satan claimed his love extended only as far as God's blessings. His love was false, said Satan, who challenged God to withdraw the blessings. Do that, he said, and Job will curse his maker. God of course knew Job would remain true—and thus the central struggle of the story.[43]

Another picture of this comes in the form of a vision given by the prophet Zechariah. An angel showed him the high priest, Joshua. As the poor priest stood clad in filthy garments before the angel of the Lord, Satan leaned in to accuse, to say that the man was unclean, unworthy. But though the demon smeared, the angel advocated. He first rebuked the accuser and next commanded celestial attendants to provide Joshua with pure, clean garments.[44]

If we jump back to Job, we get a similar picture of the angel-advocate, "a mediator, one of the thousand, to declare to man what is right." This angel is merciful or "gracious to him, and says [to God], 'Deliver him from going down into the Pit, I have found a ransom.'" Because the angel pleads the man's cause, God now listens when the man prays and accepts him "into his presence with joy."[45] This role of the angels points to the ultimate advocate for God's people, Christ.

It's a powerful bit of contrast. The demons desire our demise, but the angels take wing in our defense. They guide us in righteousness and pray for us to God, asking that he be merciful and restore us. At the end of Job's story, after the great contest concluded with Job the victor, angels exulted in his victory. Said John Chrysostom, "the very theatre of angels shouted at beholding his fortitude of soul, and applauded him as he won his crown!"[46]

8

With the stories of God's deliverance, sometimes a more severe picture emerges, one in which angels are tasked with executing judgment. Taking the observation of Ambrose of Milan, such work makes the angels "groan."[47]

Sometimes these labors are merely the flipside of defending the faithful. The events at the Red Sea were, for instance, one thing to the Israelite and quite another to the Egyptian, but they were the same events. God's protection of his people sometimes necessitated the destruction of their enemies, often in the very same move. During the reign of King Hezekiah of Judah, for instance, an angel was sent to defend Jerusalem from the surrounding armies of the Assyrian king Sennacherib, a task he accomplished by destroying the entire Assyrian army in one night. Besieged at dusk, God's people found themselves delivered by dawn, and an angel did the work.[48]

But angels were occasionally charged with opposing God's people, too, particularly when they persisted in sin and disobedience. Take one of the more obscure stories about Moses. Sent by God to confront Pharaoh, Moses stopped en route to Egypt with his retinue and stayed at an inn. "Now it happened on the way at the lodging," says the text, "an angel of the Lord met him and was seeking to kill him."[49]

Whether the "him" was Moses or his son is not clear from the text. What's clearer is why there was trouble in the first place. Despite his role as savior of the Hebrew people and despite the centuries-old command that all Hebrew boys be circumcised as a sign of God's covenant with Abraham and his descendants, Moses, one of those descendants, had not yet circumcised his child.

It is a widely disputed passage, and many early interpreters came to different conclusions about it. Origen
seemed to think the angel was the Devil.[50] Augustine
thought the angel was from God but was sent to kill
the boy, not his father.[51] And Maximus the Confessor
thoroughly allegorized the text, basically removing any
such difficulties.[52]

For his part, Ephraim the Syrian imagined that Moses'
wife, Zipporah, had opposed the circumcision. Why,
after all, would a gentile woman—Moses did not marry
a Hebrew—want her son so subjected? She likely considered it mutilation. Ephraim suggested that the couple even
argued about it that very night. Moses acquiesced, fearing
his wife more than God, and thereby exposed his mission
as something of a sham. *Scandalous* doesn't quite capture
the thing. After all, was God's covenant with Abraham
real or not? The angel came to answer the question, and
his arrival must have been terrifying.

When Zipporah realized what was happening, she
repented, snatched up a blade of flint, and circumcised
her son before falling down at the angel's feet to plead
mercy, something explicit in the Septuagint rendering
and assumed by Ephraim in his interpretation. "I have
a husband of blood," she said, indicating Moses' obedience and the sudden absence of any reason to harm him.
The angel relented. Whatever her earlier reluctance,
Zipporah's quick action saved her family from an angel
tasked with an unfortunate job.[53]

Things turned out worse for King David. His exact sin is somewhat vague, but he seems to have violated the Mosaic prescription for conducting a census. Violation came with the threat of plague, and David did not escape.[54] God sent disaster by the hand of an angel, and some seventy thousand were killed throughout the land before God showed mercy and stayed the angel's hand. Ominously, at one point in the narrative, David looked up and saw the angel overhead, "standing between earth and heaven, and in his hand a drawn sword stretched out over Jerusalem."[55]

Angels do not relish such grim chores. "Seeing that their life is blessed," said Ambrose, "would [the angels] not rather pass it in their ancient state of tranquility than be interrupted by the infliction of vengeance on our sins? They who rejoice in the salvation of one sinner must surely groan over the miseries of so grievous sins."[56] God must surely groan as well.

9

The Lord had previously warned the Hebrews that the promised land would spew them out if they lived like their pagan neighbors. Through the generations, God struggled with Israel as with a rebellious teenager, encouraging, admonishing, disciplining. But instead of growing in faith like Abraham and Jacob, the people descended into rebellion and unbelief. In the face of persistent sins, particularly idolatry, immorality, and injustice, God finally withdrew his protection, and foreign powers had their way with them, sweeping in and scooping up the people as captives.[57]

Despite the horrible turn of events, angels still protected the faithful, those like Shadrach, Meshach, and Abednego, whose angelic guardian cooled the flames of King Nebuchadnezzar's furnace, which he had stoked especially hot for their demise.[58] God likewise sent his angel to protect Daniel in the lions' den. The angel shut the cats' snapping mouths so they could do him no harm, while another angel grabbed the prophet Habakkuk by the hair and flew him to Daniel's side to deliver the faithful prisoner a meal.[59]

More than just protectors, angels acted as guides and prophetic translators, offering insight into unfolding events. The prophet Ezekiel experienced several powerful multisensory visions. In one, he saw God's cherubic throne and heard the sound of its wings "like the sound of many waters."[60] God called him to be a "watchman" for Israel, to warn them of the coming judgments.[61] Though Ezekiel was already captive in Babylon, God wanted him to know the level of evil back in Jerusalem. As with Habakkuk, an angel clutched him by the locks and spirited him away, this time in a vision to the Holy City where he saw priests offering incense to idols, women practicing rites to the Babylonian god

Tammuz, and men worshipping the sun.[62] God ordered an angel to identify all those not worshipping idols and ordered several others to sweep through the city and kill the idolaters. After this, the cherubim mounted up and departed the Jerusalem temple with the glory of God.[63]

Daniel was exiled to Babylon a few years before Ezekiel, but they were contemporaries and suffered through the same period. Daniel earned the favor and confidence of King Nebuchadnezzar by interpreting visions and dreams, thereby securing a powerful position.[64] At one point Nebuchadnezzar dreamt of a great and fruitful tree. Visible far and wide, its branches reached to heaven, and its canopy overstretched the fields of earth. Down from heaven swept an angel, "a watcher, a holy one," who ordered the tree be hewn to the stump. "The sentence is by the decree of the watchers," said the angel, "the decision by the word of the holy ones, [so] that the living may know that the Most High rules the kingdom of men, and gives it to whom he will, and sets over it the lowliest of men."[65] *Watcher* was the Babylonian word for "angel," and it appears in later Jewish and Christian writings, denoting another function of the angels—to observe the affairs of people.

The unnerved Nebuchadnezzar called Daniel to interpret, but the prophet said nothing to settle his mind. The tree, Daniel said, was the king, and its reduction was his humiliation. It came true exactly as Daniel foretold. Nebuchadnezzar was driven mad before finally coming to repentance and restoration, a token of the blessing that would come to the nations through Abraham and Jacob.[66]

10

Some visions were too great for Daniel, particularly four fantastical and violent beasts he saw rise from the sea. While puzzling over the meaning, he suddenly found himself in the heavenly court and saw God seated on a fiery throne with wheels of fire and streaming flames, just as Ezekiel had also seen. Innumerable angels pressed around the throne to serve. One of the beasts that Daniel had seen was then killed and destroyed with fire, after which "a son of man" approached the throne and was granted everlasting authority over all the peoples of the world.[67]

Daniel approached a nearby angel to ask what it all meant. The beasts were kings, explained the angel, but true and lasting authority will be given to God's people. And the beast destroyed by fire? This was a uniquely rapacious kingdom that would oppress God's people but would eventually fall and be destroyed after the heavenly court sits in judgment. Despite the explanation, Daniel confessed, "[M]y thoughts greatly alarmed me, and my color changed."[68]

After another inexplicable vision, the angel Gabriel came to reveal the meaning. His appearance, as mentioned in chapter I, overpowered the man. After Gabriel roused the shocked and unconscious prophet and explained the vision, he told him to keep it secret because the message was for a future time. Daniel was left feeling overwhelmed, even sick, and still puzzled.[69] Thankfully Gabriel quickly returned when Daniel prayed that God would remember his promises about the Exile. Said the angel, "I have now come out to give you wisdom and understanding . . . for you are greatly beloved."[70]

A certain concern comes through in these encounters. When Gabriel next visited, for instance, he was fully frightening—all beaming, blazing fire and gleaming bronze. Daniel, petrified, passed out again. But Gabriel woke him, lifted him to his feet, and told him that he was "greatly beloved" and encouraged him, "Fear not." It wasn't enough. Daniel was still overwhelmed and mute. So the angel reached out and touched his lips, enabling him to speak, but Daniel said that he had no strength. Seeing that the poor man was overcome, the angel softened and took on, as Daniel recounted, "the appearance of a man." The more humanlike angel reached out and touched Daniel again, recalling the tender reach of Elijah's angel, and strengthened the prophet.[71]

11

Daniel was by no means the only prophet personally given insight into events by angels. Perhaps the most intriguing book in the Bible about the interaction of angels and people is that of Zechariah. From one scene to the next, an angel—Zechariah repeatedly calls him "the angel who talked with me"—reveals the meaning of various signs and occurrences.

Of particular importance is what happens in the twelfth and thirteenth chapters. It's a hint of the restoration to come. The angel of the Lord, who departed from Israel so long ago, would again go before the people of God, said the prophet, and the Lord would again protect them.[72] But the protection of God is not enough to cleanse the people of their sins; that would come from the "fountain opened" from the side of Christ, "him whom they have pierced."[73] This is the healing fountain from the wounds of Christ that will water the nations and finally fulfill the blessing of Abraham.

This Christ, as we see in the next chapter, will wage war on the demons, and his holy angels will uphold God's people through their struggles with the Devil. The second-century *Epistle to Diognetus* echoes this. To declare the gospel, God "did not, as one might suppose, send them one of his servants or an angel or a ruler or any of those who administer earthly activities or who are entrusted with heavenly affairs, but he sent the craftsman and maker of all things himself."[74] God did not send an angel. He sent the Lord of the angels.

Lord of the Angels

The Advent and Saving Work of Christ

Come, then, and chase the cruel host.
WILLIAM COWPER, *Olney Hymns*

1

The story of Christ is shot through with angels. Jesus said as much when he told Nathanael, one of his earliest followers, "[Y]ou will see heaven opened, and the angels of God ascending and descending upon the Son of man."[1] We spot them as they move first this way, then that, rung by rung throughout the gospel narrative.

Angels are the original evangelists. They "are good preachers," said Augustine in his *Homilies on the Gospel of John*, "preaching Christ." Augustine reckoned their ascent and descent as one way to understand their ministry, their activity; they move from heaven to earth to share the good news, just as Gabriel and the angels of the nativity did. Angels preached Christ, he said, "from head to foot, from the beginning even to the end."[2] They feature in Christ's ascension, his resurrection, many times during his earthly life, at his birth, and even before his conception to announce the coming good news.

2

As *The Protoevangelium of James*—a book popular among early Christians—paints the picture, an elderly man and a widower named Joseph found himself newly engaged to a young maiden. Mary had been raised from infancy in the temple. Church tradition says that while there she was fed by angels, an image that hearkens back to Israel sustained by "the bread of angels."[3] But she could not stay in the temple forever. Arrangements were made for Mary to wed Joseph.

Joseph's business required him to leave for a time shortly after their betrothal. While her future husband was away, Mary turned her attention to helping the priests weave a new veil for the temple. One day, as she worked on her portion of the job, Mary set down her scarlet and purple thread to rest and get a drink of water. That's when the angel interrupted.[4]

"Hail, full of grace," said the angel Gabriel, appearing

An icon of the Annunciation from the Church of St. Clement in Ohrid, Republic Macedonia. Though this image is from the fourteenth century, the icon "quotes" from a much earlier, original form widely reproduced over centuries and nations. The shaft of dark light coming from the top of the image is the divine presence of the Holy Spirit overshadowing Mary.

out of nowhere. Icons, manuscript illuminations, and frescoes sometimes show the angel's powerful wings open and askew, as if they were still flapping as he made his sudden entry.[5] "[T]he Lord is with you," he continued. "Blessed are you among women!"[6]

Just like the prophet Daniel before her, Mary was too terrified by Gabriel's appearance to rejoice, but the angel was quick to comfort. "Do not be afraid," he said, "for you have found favor with God." Gabriel continued, "[Y]ou will conceive in your womb and bear a son, and you shall call his name Jesus. He will be great, and will be called the Son of the Most High . . . and he will reign over the house of Jacob for ever; and of his kingdom there will be no end."[7]

Through this young woman, God intended to fulfill his promise to Abraham and bless the earth. He intended to deliver fallen humanity. By the power of the Holy Spirit, Mary would conceive and bear Jesus Christ, the anointed Savior of God's people; and unlike her rebellious forebears, Mary heard the voice of the angel and obeyed. She bowed, telling Gabriel, "Behold, I am the handmaid of the Lord; let it be to me according to your word."[8]

The archangel Gabriel has possessed a unique place in this unfolding salvation story. Not only does he bridge Old and New Testaments, first helping Daniel, but he also announced the birth of John the Baptist and forerunner to Christ, even giving his intended name to

the boy's father.[9] Afterward he cleared up the misunderstanding surrounding Mary's surprise pregnancy. When
he returned from his travels, Joseph was understandably
dismayed to see his future wife pregnant. He decided
to call off their wedding, but the angel counseled otherwise. Though unnamed in the account, the angel is
usually assumed to be Gabriel because of his proximity
to the holy family and his role in announcing the incarnation of Christ.[10]

It is both interesting and important that Gabriel
described himself as one of the angels who stands in the
presence of God.[11] We see this in the opening chapters
of Job, where the angels are said to come and go before
the throne of God, and in the book of Tobit, where the
archangel Raphael mentioned being one of seven angels
who enter the presence of God.[12] The same is echoed
in Revelation.[13] Gabriel wasn't just any angel; he was
part of a special corps of messengers. And this highly
honored messenger was given the highest-honored job,
heralding the coming of Jesus Christ, the Son of God,
who will deliver God's people from the clutches of Satan
and his fallen host.

3

Ancient Christian tradition affirms that God tasked the
angels with overseeing the nations and leading them to

knowledge of himself. Papias, bishop of Hierapolis, was a friend of the bishop and martyr Polycarp and secretary to the apostle John. He said, referring to the angels, "[God] appointed some of them . . . to rule over the administration of the earth, and he ordered them to rule it well." Unfortunately, he said, the angels failed. People were simply too rebellious and corrupt. Try as they might, the angels could not break or even slow the momentum toward evil first begun in the fall. The angelic assignment, said Papias, "came to nothing."[14]

"[T]he activity of the demons daily waxed greater," said Eusebius of Caesarea, who lived between the third and fourth centuries. Evil spirits dragged humanity deeper and deeper into delusion. As we saw in chapter 3, God's own chosen people ultimately succumbed. "[E]ven the Hebrew race was hurried along in the destruction of the godless," said Eusebius, but "at last the Savior and Physician of the Universe [came] down Himself to men, bringing reinforcement to His angels for the salvation of men."[15] Imagine then the angelic excitement, joy, and even relief when the Savior finally arrived.

And so, when Mary's child came, the skies erupted over the birthplace in Bethlehem. "At the birth of the Son," said Ephraim the Syrian in *Hymns on the Nativity*, "there was a great shouting in Bethlehem; for the angels came down and gave praise there. Their voices were a great thunder."[16]

"Glory to God in the highest," they sang, "and on

earth peace, goodwill toward men!"[17] They were joyous, said Ephraim, because "the Wakeful came to wake us!"[18]

But this peace was a promise. It was not yet actual, not yet real. The peace would come only after a great battle. As Origen said in his *Commentary on the Gospel of John*, "[T]he angels also wonder at the peace which is to be brought about on account of Jesus on the earth, that seat of war, on which Lucifer, star of the morning, fell from heaven, to be warred against and destroyed by Jesus."[19] The advent of Jesus threatened to undo all of Satan's work. Because of this, from the moment of his birth, danger loomed for the savior child.

4

Pick up the story from a different vantage point:

> And a great portent appeared in heaven, a woman clothed with the sun, with the moon under her feet, and on her head a crown of twelve stars; she was with child and she cried out in her pangs of birth, in anguish for delivery. And another portent appeared in heaven; behold, a great red dragon, with seven heads and ten horns, and seven diadems upon his heads. His tail swept down a third of the stars of heaven, and cast them to the earth. And the dragon stood before the woman who was about to bear

a child, that he might devour her child when she brought it forth.[20]

The woman is Mary. She is Israel, the church. She is the faithful people of God through whom Christ came into the world and to destroy the works of the Devil. The clash began at the birth of Jesus when Satan, the dragon, tried to destroy his infant foe.

To achieve his aim, the Devil employed the services of the fearful and hateful King Herod. Upon news of Christ's birth, Herod reenacted ancient Pharaoh's mass infanticide and ordered the deaths of all male children, two years old and under, in the region of Bethlehem.[21] The king crouched gape-mawed before the woman to devour her child, but the pair escaped. An angel—likely Gabriel, but the text is again silent on his identity—warned Joseph about Herod's homicidal plan and instructed him to flee to Egypt with Mary and Jesus.[22]

In writing his gospel, Matthew calls Pharaoh and Egypt to mind on purpose. As with Jacob and the people of Israel, an angel went before Christ and protected him. This starts a string of events that Matthew uses to link Christ to ancient Israel—not only the flight to Egypt to avoid calamity, but even the departure, which was prompted and led by the angel.[23]

With angelic aid, Christ accomplished his own exodus and returned to Palestine for his own conquest of the Holy Land—a New Israel to finish what the first did not. Only, instead of Canaanites, Christ conquered the demons in the land. With Jesus' birth, as Cyril of Alexandria preached, "the power of the devil was spoiled. For . . . he had been the object of religious service, and had . . . very many worshippers; but when the holy virgin brought forth, the power of his tyranny was broken."[24]

To commence his ministry Jesus was baptized in the Jordan by his cousin John and then ventured into the wilderness to fast and pray for forty days, a time that hearkened back to the Israelites' forty-year wilderness journey. As the Israelites were faced with temptation, so was this New Israel.[25]

Following the fast, Satan approached and tempted Jesus three separate times: first, to assuage his hunger by turning stones to bread; second, to throw himself off the temple, knowing that angels would stop his fall; and third, to fall down and worship Satan in exchange for power over all the world. Jesus rebuffed each and every temptation and finally commanded his adversary to leave: "Begone, Satan! for it is written, 'You shall worship the Lord your God, and him only shall you serve.'"[26] The beaten Devil then withdrew "until an opportune time," as the text says, to regroup for another assault.[27] Christ weathered the conflict, prevailing where Israel had previously failed. And at that point, according to Matthew's gospel, "angels came and ministered to him."[28]

This is a mystery of sorts. Commenting on Psalm 57, Augustine shed light from the verse, "He hath sent from heaven and hath saved me." David's psalm foreshadowed the passion of Christ, a fact that Augustine unpacked in his commentary, here seeing that God sent his angels down to Christ to "save him" after the Temptation. But the angels, said Augustine, ministered "not like men merciful to one indigent, but like subjects to One Omnipotent."[29]

Icons of Jesus' baptism often show John the Baptist on one bank of the Jordan with a clutch of angels on the other. The angels are typically shown with veiled hands, a sign of respect and care, as if the person or thing they might handle were too prized to touch bare-handed.[30] If we imagine these same angels as those that descended after the Temptation, their disposition comes into view. They were not waiting on an invalid; they were serving their Lord. Nor was it the last time they would so minister. But in the meantime, Jesus took the fight to the demons.

5

After picking the first of his disciples, Jesus went to Capernaum and taught in the synagogue, where he encountered a demon-possessed man. "Let us alone!" cried the demons, startled and tormented by the presence of Christ. "Did You come to destroy us?" they asked, but Jesus offered no response. He simply ordered the demons to be quiet and then exorcised them with one command: "[C]ome out of him!" To the astonishment of all around, the spirits obeyed.[31]

It was only the start. Jesus' ministry was marked by many such events, perhaps most dramatically in the case of the Gadarene demoniac when he cast some thousand demons out of a man and into a herd of pigs. The animals became so frantic and crazed by the experience that they raced off a cliff into the sea. The down-slope scurry frightened the townsfolk to the point they pleaded with Jesus to leave.[32]

Even the healing ministry of Jesus involved this battle against dark forces. The reason that Christ restored physical health is that in some sense and to some extent the physical infirmity he encountered was the result of demonic activity. So we find Jesus healing people afflicted by demons that made them mute and blind.[33] Likewise, we find him verbally rebuking the fever of disciple Simon Peter's mother-in-law and then healing many others, some of whom had demons flee with their afflictions. And we find him driving out "a spirit of infirmity" that caused a woman to suffer nearly twenty years hunched over and bent; in her case Jesus specifically said that her disability was caused by the Devil.[34]

While Jesus set many people free, the Gadarene

locals weren't the only ones uneasy with his activities. The Jewish religious leaders were beginning to worry as well. At least twice the Pharisees accused Jesus of casting out demons by the power of Beelzebul (or Baalzebub, the prince of demons we first encountered in the previous chapter). On one of these occasions, Jesus rebuked the naysayers. "[I]f Satan casts out Satan," he said, "he is divided against himself; how then will his kingdom stand? . . . But if it is by the Spirit of God that I cast out demons, then the kingdom of God has come upon you."[35]

Indeed, it had. And it was plain to all, depending on how much light God granted them. It is telling that the demon in Capernaum exclaimed to know Christ's identity: "I know who you are!"[36] As Christ walked humbly among humans, his stride simultaneously struck awe and fear. "Visibly children surrounded Him in the street; secretly angels surrounded Him in fear," hymned Ephraim the Syrian. "Cheerful was He with the little ones as a child; awful was He with the angels as a Commander"—*awful* in the old sense of filling one with awe. "The angels as angels saw Him," said Ephraim, which is to say they surrounded and served one they recognized as the Son of God. "[A]ccording to the measure of his knowledge each man beheld Him."[37]

For the demons, that meant they scurried and ran before the face of a conqueror. The liberator had arrived, and humanity's demonic oppressors were on the run.

6

Significantly Jesus involved others in his mission. He not only called disciples to follow and learn from him, but he also sent them into other areas to replicate and extend his work. Jesus gave his disciples "authority over unclean spirits [demons], to cast them out, and to heal every disease and every infirmity," as it says in Matthew's gospel. The disciples were to preach that the kingdom of heaven was at hand. They were, said Jesus, to "[h]eal the sick, raise the dead, cleanse leapers, [and] cast out demons."[38] All these actions were of a piece—the overturning of Satan's control of humanity. He sent out seventy such disciples, a number that corresponds to the number of angelic princes over the nations. Ancient Christian commentators like Cyril of Alexandria understood this action as revealing Christ's intent to liberate all the peoples of the world.[39]

After a time the disciples returned successful and excited by their accomplishments. "Lord," they said to Jesus, "even the demons are subject to us in your name!" Upon hearing the news, Jesus was quick to tell them to "rejoice that your names are written in heaven," not because "spirits are subject to you."[40] After all, if their focus was on "work[ing] miracles, and crush[ing] the herds of demons," said Cyril, they might fall prey to "the desire also of vainglory," whose nearest neighbor is pride. "Most usefully, therefore, does the Savior of all rebuke the first boasting."[41] What use would it be to cast out demons if the disciples became puffed up just the same?[42]

In the same encounter Jesus directed the disciples to the cosmic scope of his mission, the same mission to which he called them: "I saw Satan fall like lightning from heaven."[43] As Jesus' disciples went out, they were actively participating in the destruction of Satan's kingdom. Satan, commented Cyril, "was cast down from on high to earth: from overweening pride to humiliation: from glory to contempt: from great power to utter weakness. . . . [B]ecause the Only-begotten Word of God has come down from heaven, he has fallen like lightning."[44]

Take up the story again from the vantage point of heaven, as we find it in Revelation. After the dragon's failed attempt at devouring the woman's child, John wrote that

> war broke out in heaven: Michael and his angels fought with the dragon; and the dragon and his angels fought, but they did not prevail, nor was a place found for them in heaven any longer. So the great dragon was cast out, that serpent of old, called the Devil and Satan, who deceives the whole world; he was cast to the earth, and his angels were cast out with him.[45]

This passage in Revelation is sometimes applied to

the original fall of Satan, which we covered here in chapter 2, but since it immediately follows the birth of the
child, who is clearly Christ, it seems to fit better as the
heavenly side of the earthly conflict between the city of
God and the city of the world at the time of Christ's
ministry on earth. Not that the other interpretation is
strictly wrong. It is fair to say that the fall of Satan is as
much a recurring motif as a singular event.

7

Following his triumphal entry into Jerusalem, Jesus
announced, "Now is the judgment of this world, now
shall the ruler of this world be cast out."[46] The image is
clear: the rightful king has arrived to oust his pretender.

But the imposter would not go easily. Once Jesus
entered the city, confrontations increased, tensions
mounted, and the conflict reached a fever pitch. Some of
Jesus' very own disciples became casualties. Satan, said
Jesus, using a frightful image, wanted to sift his lead
disciple like wheat.[47] Peter survived, despite a tempo-
rary betrayal of Christ, but another of Jesus' men, Judas,
betrayed him to the uttermost. Before Judas sold out the
Lord, the apostle John said with terrifying abruptness,
"Satan entered into him."[48]

Like Satan's sin, Judas's basic sin was envy and
ingratitude, something the Gospels make clear. He was

greedy, and his envy stands in sharp relief when a woman anointed Jesus with valuable perfumed oil. He wanted the money for himself. John said that Judas made a habit of pilfering cash from the disciples' common purse.[49] As a result, one of the liturgical hymns of the church refers to Judas as the "ingrate disciple."[50]

After the Last Supper, Jesus went to the Garden of Gethsemane. There he wrestled to the point of bloody tears with the agonizing path before him, facing certain and quick-pending death. This was Satan's more "opportune time," the crucial moment, the excruciating moment. To support and uphold Jesus, angels rushed to his side just as they had done in the wilderness.[51] "[H]ere all mouths, celestial and terrestrial, are insufficient to give thanks to Him by Whose hand the angels were created," commented Ephraim the Syrian; "that He was strengthened for the sakes of sinners by that angel who was created by His hand. As then the angel from above stood in glory and in brightness, while the Lord of the angel, that He might exalt man who was degraded, stood in degradation and humility."[52]

After praying, Jesus got up and, as it were, welcomed the traitor Judas and the temple guards, who were just then arriving to arrest him. The disciples there were understandably frightened, but Jesus told them it was all part of the Scripture's fulfillment. If that were not the case, he could call legions of angels to his side; and considering the damage only one angel wreaked upon the

Assyrian army, that was saying something. As the angels had comforted him, he comforted his followers with the thought of angels. Jesus could have sprung them all right there, but instead he chose the infinitely harder path. He chose the cross.

8

Icons of the Crucifixion often show angels—two, sometimes four or more, flying around the cross. Like the angels of the baptism, they usually have their hands covered. Some show the angels covering their eyes as well. The spectacle of their Lord dying such a terrible death was unbearable.[53]

But at last the thing was done. The abuse and torment of crucifixion accomplished their end, and Christ was dead. But things were not as they appeared to the weeping disciples who wrenched the nails loose from the wood and took their Lord's lifeless body to bury. In the sometimes controversial language of the Apostles' Creed, Jesus "descended into hell." Not as victim—much to the surprise of Satan, who no doubt thought he'd finally secured his long-sought triumph—but as victor.

There in the realm of the dead, Christ blasted through Satan's gates like a battering ram. Prudentius painted the scene in his collection of poems, *The Daily Round*: "The door [of hell] is forced and yields before

Him; the bolts are torn away, down falls the pivot broken; that gate so ready to receive the inrush, so unyielding in face of those that would return, is unbarred and gives back the dead."[54]

Satan never saw it coming. Christ bound the strong man, raided his house, and liberated the captives.[55] A classic depiction of the Resurrection shows Christ ascending from the grave, Hades' doors broken and lying in a crosswise pattern as the Lord takes Adam and Eve by the wrist—taking all of fallen humanity by the wrist—and frees them from their age-old imprisonment to death and the Devil. Often these same scenes show angels aloft, their hands draped in reverence, while an old man, Satan, is bound beneath the feet of the risen Christ.[56] Ephraim the Syrian put these words on the lips of the Devil: "By the nails which he received, He made me to suffer. I rejoiced when I crucified Him: and I knew not that He was crucifying me, in His crucifixion."[57]

Christ, the Lord and giver of life, could not be kept in the grave once he had defeated death and the Devil. On the morning of the Resurrection, an earthquake shook the ground. But nothing shook the guards at Christ's tomb as much as seeing a radiant, gleaming angel descend from the sky and roll back the tombstone before sitting upon the rock. The guards quivered and, in the words of Matthew, "became like dead men."[58] The same angel—could it have been Gabriel again?—told

The Ascension *from the Rabbula Gospels, an illuminated gospel book created near the end of the sixth century by the monk Rabbula at his monastery in Beth Zagba, Syria. The scene depicts the Lord ascending in glory, seated upon the cherubim, angels flanking him at all sides. Angels midair carry Eucharistic loaves—something we'll explore in more detail in chapter 6—while angels on earth explain what is taking place. Despite the angelic witness, the final chapter of Matthew's gospel records that some did not believe (v. 17).*

the women disciples who had come to anoint Christ's body that he'd risen from the dead.

The risen Christ stayed with the apostles for several weeks thereafter to prepare them for furthering his work, but then it was time for his return to the Father, the moment known as the Ascension. Angels stood among the on-gazing disciples as Christ ascended and disappeared in a cloud, explaining that he would come again in the clouds.[59] Christ's story commenced with the announcement of an angel and concludes much the same.

9

The ministry of Christ broke the primordial fall of humanity. It reversed the Curse under which we lived and freed us from the dominion of sin, death, the Devil, and all the Devil's angels. But how do we participate in that victory? How do we ensure that we are on the right side of his triumph?

When the Pharisee Nicodemus came at night to inquire of Christ about the kingdom, Jesus told him, as John recorded in his gospel, "unless one is born of water and the Spirit, he cannot enter the kingdom of God."[60] The ancient church usually baptized people at Easter, and because of John's place in the lectionary, the regular cycle of scriptural readings, this story was primarily read and studied following Easter, immediately after initiates rose dripping clean from the laver. In that context, none could miss the point of Jesus' statement to Nicodemus.

While some Christians might today place little stress on baptism, it would be impossible to overestimate the importance that early Christians placed on it. The baptismal font recalled the divided waters of Jordan, through which the Israelites entered the promised land. It also hearkened back to the cleft waves of the Red Sea, through which God's people escaped the pursuit of Pharaoh and his army.[61] An angel of God served Israel at that pivotal moment of liberation, and the same is true as every person turns his back on the Devil and enters the kingdom of God and his angels.

"There cannot . . . be any doubt that before a man is reborn in Christ he is held close in the power of the devil," penned John the Deacon in the year 500, "and unless he is extricated from the devil's toils, renouncing him among the first beginnings of faith with a true confession, he cannot approach the grace of the saving laver."[62] John served in the church at Rome at the turn of the sixth century, but this idea of being liberated from Satan's clutches as part of entering the kingdom of heaven is basic and universal in ancient Christianity, going back as far as we have records.

As part of our baptisms, Christians make both professions and renunciations. "When entering the water," said Tertullian near the end of the second century, "we make profession of the Christian faith," and "we bear public testimony that we have renounced the devil, his pomp, and his angels."[63] The same formula can be found with very little variation throughout Palestine, Syria, North Africa, Byzantium, and Rome. In another instance, Tertullian used the word *disown* for the same action.[64] We declare for all ears that we no longer identify in any way with the Devil. Our identity is now in Christ; we now belong to him.

Part of this renunciation involves exorcism—prayers offered by bishops, priests, and deacons to drive away demons. In the ancient church the prayers varied depending on the time and place, but they were substantially the same and offered for the same reason. Before entering the lifesaving waters, new believers must be liberated from hell's hold on their hearts and bodies. Catechumens stand like refugees at the threshold of the kingdom, looking for liberation and sanctuary.

One early testimony to the practice of exorcism can be found in the *Apostolic Tradition*, usually attributed to Hippolytus of Rome in the year 215. Typically a time was set aside before baptism to make sure the professions of catechumens were genuine. During that time, according to Hippolytus, "a hand is laid upon them daily whilst they are exorcized."[65] In the service itself the person to be baptized was anointed with special oil:

> And when the presbyter takes hold of each of those
> who are to be baptized he should bid him renounce

saying: "I renounce you Satan, and all your service and all your works."

And when he has renounced all this he [the priest] should anoint him with the oil of exorcism saying to him: "Let all evil spirits depart far from you."[66]

Comparable versions of the rite can be found throughout the ancient church, West and East, from Ireland to Iraq. But its ubiquity shouldn't lessen the beauty and wonder of what it means—or of what transpires behind the gossamer veil of this material life.

10

In his famous *Catechetical Lectures*, Cyril of Jerusalem told those coming forward to be baptized, "[E]ach one of you is about to be presented to God before tens of thousands of the angelic hosts."[67]

The hosts are eager. The Scriptures speak of our salvation as a mystery into which the angels long to peer.[68] Though unable to fully comprehend the mystery, the angels thrill at our salvation. They rejoice with God every time a person crosses from darkness to light.[69] Gregory Nazianzen said that God "calls together his angel friends . . . and makes them sharers of His joy."[70] They even dance around us, according to Cyril.[71]

"The angels and watchers rejoice over that which is born of the Spirit and the water," affirmed Ephraim the Syrian; "they rejoice by fire and by the Spirit [that] the corporeal have become spiritual. The seraphim who sing 'holy' rejoice, that they who are made holy have increased." The angels exult that "Baptism is bringing forth the heavenly from the earthly."[72]

What enters the water as mere flesh emerges as spiritual. What was merely earthly becomes now heavenly. Flesh and spirit, earth and heaven—as they were first rejoined in Christ so they are now joined in those who put on Christ. It's a brilliant, amazing transformation worthy of deep contemplation. To that end, Cyril instructed catechumens to

lift up the eye of the mind: even now imagine the choirs of angels, and God the Lord of all there sitting, and His Only-begotten Son sitting with Him on His right hand, and the Spirit present with them; and thrones and dominions doing service, and every man of you and every woman receiving salvation. Even now let your ears ring, as it were, with that glorious sound, when over your salvation the angels shall chant, *Blessed are they whose iniquities are forgiven, and whose sins are covered*: when like stars of the Church you shall enter in, bright in the body and radiant in the soul.[73]

11

If the angels beam with the light of Christ, then we who put on Christ at baptism do as well. A scene in the Old Testament foreshadows this reality, one we looked at briefly in the previous chapter. Zechariah presents the image of the high priest Joshua "standing before the angel of the LORD, and Satan standing at his right hand to accuse him." The Lord is having none of it. He rebukes Satan, referring to Joshua as a "brand plucked from the fire." But despite the Lord's intervention, Joshua has a problem: he's filthy, dressed in dirty clothes.

The solution is already in play. The angel orders his attendants to remove the priest's clothing and then says to Joshua, "Behold, I have taken your iniquity away from you, and I will clothe you with rich apparel."[74] It's the approximate scene of our individual baptisms. Satan is thrown down and can no longer accuse us.[75] Freed from his clutches, we enter the kingdom, freshly garbed with angelic robes.

The baptismal gown is white to signal what has happened to the soul. "Your garments glisten . . . as snow," said Ephraim, "and fair is your shining in the likeness of angels."[76] "The lowly one," he said, "that has put on the Giver of greatness in the water, even though he be base in the sight of fools, yet is great in the sight of the watchers for that he is clad in greatness."[77]

In baptism we are not only joined to Christ; we are also joined to all who are joined to Christ, the entire church, including the angels. We leave one city and become members of another, a glorious city, the city of God, the kingdom of heaven. We move from darkness to light, and by that light we see an ever-expanding crowd of new friends, new neighbors, new siblings. Through the waters of baptism, said Ephraim, we are "joined with the spirits that minister to the Godhead!"[78]

We will need the host of heaven if we are to withstand the onslaught of the Enemy. The church recognizes our need for protection and aid given our state of open rebellion to the evil one. Just as when Elisha was surrounded by enemies but also surrounded by a greater number of angels, so said Ephraim, "let baptism be unto you a camp of guardians."[79] And not just an entire camp, but particularly one assigned to each of us individually.

Let us turn now to contemplate our guardian angels.

Guardians of Soul
and Body

Christians and Our Angelic Guides and Protectors

Angels and ministers of grace defend us!
SHAKESPEARE, *Hamlet*

1

As a young man in the early part of the fourth century, Macarius of Egypt was forced into unwanted marriage by his father. Though he was the son of a priest and himself a deacon, Macarius left home and took work driving camels. The job both covered the material needs of his unwanted bride and kept him as far from her side as he could reasonably manage—fulfilling one matrimonial obligation while, as it were, shirking another.

As his biography relates, one night while on the road, he fell asleep and envisioned a man "standing above him in a garment that cast forth lightning and was multicolored and striped."[1] Another version of the story identifies the visiting angel as a cherub.[2] The cherub came with a message from God and guidance about his future. Almost immediately upon his returning home, Macarius's wife succumbed to a tragic illness, and the young husband found himself a widower. Thereafter he devoted his life to prayer and asceticism.

The particulars are of course particular, but Macarius does not represent a special case. Recalling the earlier story of Elisha and the angelic army, Ambrose made an interesting comment about awareness. While Elisha sensed and even saw the encircling angels, his servant could not. Why? Ambrose pointed to the man's servile status but spiritualized it to say that the man's mind was in bondage.[3] An icon of Macarius shows him standing side by side with a mysterious red, winged figure—his cherub guide, his angelic guard. If we had the free eyes of faith, we would see ourselves also standing side by side with winged guides and guardians.

2

After the exorcism prayers in the Byzantine baptismal rite, the priest prays that God would "unite [the catechumen's] life with a shining angel."[4] Some translations of the service put it more poetically—for example, "yoke unto him a radiant angel." Whatever the phrasing, the prayer testifies to the ancient Christian conviction that every believer goes through life with a guardian angel. In the church's liturgical prayers, he's commonly referred to as "a messenger of peace, a faithful guide, a guardian of our souls and bodies."[5] The formula is so ancient that Christians have been praying it weekly, even daily, practically as long as there have been Christians.

Guardian angels are merely the particularization of Paul's understanding from Hebrews, that angels are "ministering spirits, sent forth to serve, for the sake of those who are to obtain salvation."[6] A guardian angel is sent by God to serve for *our* sakes.

That the prayer for a guardian angel is made at baptism does not preclude the presence of guardian angels in the lives of the unbaptized. Angels, to repeat, serve the heirs of salvation, and one could surmise that such include even those who are not as yet part of the church. Cornelius the centurion might well exemplify this. A man who feared God but who had not yet heard the gospel, he was directed by an angel to send for the apostle Peter, so Peter could share the gospel and baptize him.[7] Even before Cornelius's baptism, his angel was looking out for him. Angelic assistance is, according to Gregory of Nyssa, "manifested and made known whenever we apply ourselves to diligent training in the higher life," something to which we uniquely commit in baptism, but it is nonetheless "already there at our birth."[8]

The image of the guardian angel goes all the way back to the opening book of the Bible when Jacob referenced "the angel who has redeemed me from all evil."[9] Jacob received intimations of divine protection by angels on more than one recorded occasion. And there are other references throughout the Scriptures, some of which we've already seen. Psalm 34.7, for instance, promises angelic protection for those who love and obey God: "The angel of the LORD encamps around those who fear him, and delivers them." And Psalm 91 famously promises that God "will give his angels charge of you to guard you in all your ways. On their hands," the text continues, "they will bear you up, lest you dash your foot against a stone."[10]

Likewise, the book of Tobit presents us with an account of the archangel Raphael traveling with the young man Tobias as he journeys to gather a sum of money for his needful father, Tobit. The angel sees him through physical danger and spiritual danger as well, preparing Tobias for a battle with a demon that had already claimed the lives of many men.[11]

The angels' protective role is again seen in the Gospels, when Jesus pulls a child to him to settle a dispute among the disciples about who was greatest in the kingdom of heaven. "See that you do not despise one of these little ones," he says; "for I tell you that in heaven their angels always behold the face of my Father."[12] The implication is clear enough. Each of these children has an angel who watches over him or her and has the ear of God. The promise of Scripture—and therefore the expectation of believers—is that God sends his angels to guide, deliver, and protect.

3

The lives of the apostles evidence this over and again. If angels ascended and descended upon the Son of Man, if Christ drew heaven and earth together, if he empowered his disciples to further his ministry, then we should expect to encounter many angels in their stories. And so we do.

After spending time in Samaria, for instance, Philip the Evangelist was led by the verbal command of an angel to a place where he would meet a court official from Ethiopia, a man who—after being baptized by Philip's hand—in turn evangelized his own country.[13]

The book of Acts is barely under way before the apostles are arrested and thrown in jail for preaching the gospel. "But," wrote Luke, "at night an angel of the Lord opened the prison doors and brought them out and said, 'Go and stand in the temple and speak to the people all the words of this Life.'"[14] Though it doesn't say, Peter was undoubtedly part of this group, and he would soon find himself in straits more dire than these.

King Herod came after the apostles. As it says in Revelation, "the dragon . . . [made] war on the rest of [the woman's] offspring, on those who keep the commandments of God and bear testimony to Jesus."[15] Herod first killed James, the brother of John, and then he jailed Peter. But before Herod could do worse, Peter's angel fouled the king's plan.

Asleep in his cell at night, Peter did not at first wake when the angel arrived with a glow. The angel, said Luke, "struck Peter on the side and woke him, saying, 'Get up quickly.'" Just then Peter's chains fell from his hands. The angel commanded him to wrap his cloak around himself and follow. He did and walked right out of the jail, unobstructed. The pair passed one guard and then another with a locked door springing open on its own. The whole episode was so surreal Peter thought he was dreaming. Finally back in the city, the angel vanished, and Peter realized it was no dream. "Now," he said, "I am sure that the Lord has sent his angel and rescued me."[16]

The story, interestingly enough, doesn't end with the angelic jailbreak. It includes an almost comic conclusion. Peter sneaked back to the house of Mary, the mother of Mark, who later wrote the gospel that bears his name. The house was crowded with people praying for Peter and about the persecution. Peter knocked at the door. A young woman named Rhoda came to answer and recognized his voice through the door. But the overexcited girl didn't open it. She instead ran to tell the others—who didn't believe her. They were convinced Peter was probably dead, just like James. So there was Peter, a fugitive standing outside, pounding on the door, and inside the house the disbelievers were telling Rhoda, "You are mad." She kept after it, but they only responded, "It is his angel!" What about that frantic knocking? They finally checked, "and when they opened, they saw [Peter] and were amazed."[17] Better than just a humorous moment, the passage also demonstrates the belief that people had particular angels assigned to them, angels that possibly even resemble their charges.[18]

Paul had the assistance of angels as well. When Paul sailed for Rome, the voyage met with rough storms and tempestuous seas. At one point the passage was imperiled by winds so severe and waves so high, the voyagers feared for their lives. But not Paul. His guardian angel appeared to him and told him not to fear. "[Y]ou must stand before Caesar," he said; "and lo, God has granted you all those who sail with you."[19] Whatever the worry, however dire the circumstances, Paul was not going to go down in that ship. God had other plans.

On this same point, compare the imprisonments of Peter and Paul. An angel sprang Peter, but Paul's angel—who would later personally comfort him in a storm—left him in his cell. Why? Chrysostom answered that "God disposes all things in divers ways" and notes that in Paul's case "the jailer was to be converted."[20] Had Paul escaped, the jailer would have killed himself and never heard the gospel. In both cases the outcome served those who were to obtain salvation.

In all of these stories, it's clear that without angelic intervention the gospel would not have gone forward; either someone would have failed to hear it (Cornelius or the Ethiopian), or the evangelists themselves would have been killed (Peter and Paul).

4

The view that guardian angels attend us is grounded in passages like those we've already seen and the teaching of the ancient church. For instance, John Chrysostom, commenting on the passage about Peter's angelic jail-break, said, "This is a truth, that each man has an angel."[21] In his book *On the Holy Spirit*, Basil the Great likewise spoke of angels being "tutors and teachers arranged for men" and "those . . . entrusted with the care of souls."[22]

The early Christians universally believed that our angels are present in our lives and attend to our needs, encouraging us, praying for us, protecting us, even implanting godly thoughts in our hearts and minds.

In chapter I, I mentioned that people may have

passing impressions or certain moods that suddenly come upon them. Sometimes these are angelic. Hermas of Rome spoke about "the angel of righteousness" who provokes in our hearts thoughts of "righteousness, purity, reverence, contentment, every upright deed, and every glorious virtue."[23] If angels serve for the sake of our salvation, we should expect as much. Human sanctification requires outside assistance. While the Holy Spirit speaks to our hearts, assistance also comes from our guardian angels, probably much more than we realize.

Clement of Alexandria dwelled on this a bit in his *Miscellanies.* "[T]he thoughts of virtuous men are produced through the inspiration of God," he said, adding that "particular divine ministers" contribute to "the divine will being conveyed to human souls." These particular divine ministers are the angels, some of whom are assigned to nations and cities, and others who are "assigned to individuals." These angels encourage us as we grow in knowledge and incline our minds and hearts ever closer to divine understanding and wisdom. "For by angels," he added, "the divine power bestows good things."[24]

Gregory Thaumaturgus, born 213, spoke of "those beings who are not seen, but yet are more godlike [than people], and who have a special care for men." About his own guardian angel, Gregory said that he was "allotted to [the angel] from my boyhood to rule, and rear, and train." This celestial teacher, given by God, "fed me from my youth," he said, and "still at this present time sustains, and instructs, and conducts me."[25]

Being conducted implies receiving guidance, direction, even companionship along the journey of life. This is precisely the picture that we get with Macarius of Egypt and his guardian cherub. Macarius's cherub visited him many times during his life. Humorously he came once to chide his ward for ignoring an earlier direction, the one that launched him on the monastic life. "Why are you so obtuse?" the angel asked, evidently annoyed. But he also encouraged Macarius, instructing him on his mission, strengthening his resolve against temptation, consoling him after battles with demons, and assuring him of God's presence.[26]

Beyond seeing us through our life's journey, angels are used by God to orchestrate certain events along that journey. We experience nothing by chance, and Isaac the Syrian said in his *Ascetical Homilies* that our guardian angels actually take part in managing the so-called "accidental occurrences" of our lives. God intends trials and testing as tools for teaching and training, and angels participate in his plans for us. "There is a guardian with each one of us, whose notice nothing escapes and who never weakens. But all occurrences are very carefully managed by this appointed guardian."[27] If we take our trials as training, then our guardian angels assume the place of coaches, helping us get through the moment, urging us on, praying for us, even arranging the circumstances for our victory if we respond as God desires. If we seek to fulfill God's will, said Isaac elsewhere, we will "have the angels of heaven as [our] guide."[28]

Given this level of intimacy and care, it's inconceivable that the assignment of guardian angels would be random or willy-nilly. Gregory Thaumaturgus, for instance, suggested that angels are assigned by a "momentous decision."[29] Given our particular needs and singular dispositions, we need an angel just as particular and singular to match. We've already seen certain symmetry between people and the angels, something Scripture leads us to contemplate. Add to that a certain complementarity. Just consider the assumption behind the statement that Peter's voice outside Mary's door really belonged to his angel *because it sounded like him*. We're closer than we think, paired at some certain and significant level.

We are paired with an angel individually suited to our personal pursuit of salvation. "[W]e are not to imagine that [the angels] obtained these offices otherwise than by their own [individual] merits," remarked Origen, "and by the zeal and excellent qualities which they severally demonstrated." Origen's speculation makes perfectly good sense. Angels are individuals. Angels, furthermore, have social structure and hierarchy, facts that testify to their differences and variances in position and place, even person. Origen's point is simply that God uses this diversity to our advantage—a sort of heavenly division of labor. Whether it's the angel to whom the Ephesian church was corporately entrusted, the angel similarly over the Smyrneans, or those individually with Peter, Paul, and Cornelius, each is paired with his charge "agreeably to the merits and good qualities and mental vigor of each individual spirit."[30]

Our angels are not randomly assigned. They are matched with us because they are the best match for us.

5

In that same passage from Origen, he mentioned the ominous fact that we find not only good angels with us, but also bad.

With the giving of the Law, a choice was presented to Israel: the path of blessings, God's way, or that of cursings, the Devil's. And more clearly now than ever there was, in a very real sense, a contest for the soul of man. Israel was the new Adam and Eve, and the fruit was again laid before them. On the one hand, an angel encouraged obedience. On the other, a demon prompted rebellion. "God and his angels call us toward life," wrote Macarius of Alexandria (not to be confused with the other Macarius from whom we've already heard), "but the evil one and his host desire our perdition."[31]

The idea of an angel on one shoulder and a demon on the other was not born from cartoons or pop culture.

It goes back to ancient times. Take the second-century *Epistle of Barnabas* for one example: "There are two paths of teaching and authority, the path of light and the path of darkness. And the difference between the two paths is great. For over the one are appointed light-bearing angels of God, but over the other angels of Satan."[32]

"A person has two angels," said Hermas of Rome, "one of righteousness and the other of wickedness."[33]

John Cassian repeated the thought. "Scripture bears witness that two angels, a good and a bad one, cling to each one of us," he reported.[34] What scripture? Cassian cited Psalm 34.7 and Matthew 18.10 about angels delivering the faithful and watching over children. As for the demon on the other shoulder, Cassian cited Hermas, which was considered part of the Scripture by many in the early church. He also cited Satan's tempting of Job, as well as the Psalter: "And let the devil stand at his right hand."[35] Man is pictured between these two influences, capable of choosing the right or the wrong. It is within our "power to make the one prevail over the other," said Gregory of Nyssa.[36]

This choice is not presented as a dualistic affair with light and dark in perpetual battle. Early Christian writers denounced such views as pagan and alien to the approach they received from Christ and the apostles. This is not an equal battle between light and dark. Satan swept a third of the stars from heaven, not all, not even half. God, not Satan, is almighty. Heaven outweighs, overpowers, and upstages hell at every turn. Satan may be the illegitimate prince of this world, but God is the rightful lord of all things seen and unseen.[37] By cooperating with the grace of God given in Christ, humans can really defeat the Devil and his demons.

And what's more, with Satan's defeat in the resurrection, his power is radically curbed. But that doesn't mean Christians are without battles to wage.

6

According to *The Ladder of Divine Ascent* by seventh-century monastic guide John Climacus, we fall under spiritual and satanic attack when we are prideful, when we are negligent of responsibilities (whether spiritual or material), and when the demons turn their envy on us.[38] The first two are pitfalls that we can avoid by cultivating humility and self-discipline, but the last is one that we can only pray to overcome by personal endurance and outside deliverance. Thankfully our guardian angels provide such deliverance or strengthen us for the fight to endure if God desires that we weather the attack.

The demons cannot read our minds, but neither are Satan and his angels bereft of wiles and cunning. Macarius of Alexandria said our thoughts project from our minds like branches from a tree trunk. Just as a man climbing a tree can only grab two or three branches at any given time, Satan can only grasp two or three of our thoughts. "A few of these Satan can know," said Macarius, "but the rest he does not even perceive."[39] He and the demons can test and tempt and poke and prod—all the while carefully observing our reactions to see if we will succumb to sin.

Demons are expert at leveraging our weaknesses. When we are tired or ill, they prompt us to be angry, irritable, or short-tempered. When we're distracted by ease and wealth, they prompt us toward indulgence, gluttony, and fornication. When we are alone or separated from loved ones, they prompt us toward doubts, carelessness, and despondency.[40]

But our guardian angels are given for our defense. The early writers saw these angels as drawn and encouraged by our prayers and our efforts to lead holy lives. If we persist in pursuing God, humbling ourselves, and growing in grace, they desire nothing more than to protect and defend us from our spiritual foes. The Devil, said Isaac the Syrian, "cannot withstand the angel who strengthens and helps the man."[41]

Sometimes the angels assist us amid the trial. Climacus said that the demons buffet us while we sleep, but we awake feeling good and peaceful because "we are secretly encouraged by the holy angels."[42] Most of us are more aware of our waking struggles, and for these, according to Isaac the Syrian, our guardian angels provide "strength and patience."[43] When we choose to oppose the Devil, said Gregory of Nyssa, "[t]hen [our] brother brings [us] assistance and joins [us], for the angel, who in a way is a brother . . . appears . . . and stands by us."[44]

The Scripture says that God will not test us beyond our abilities to resist.[45] Where we are particularly weak, our angels may help provide escape. Evagrius, as an example, was captured by lustful thoughts of a married woman with whom he had contact. He was arrogant, and because of his pride, his biography explains, "he fell into the hand of the demon that causes lustful thoughts." For the sake of his soul, the contact with the woman needed to cease immediately. But Evagrius was a sucker for her allure and advances. Despite his prayers, he felt powerless to resist and was too cowardly to flee, as Joseph had done with Potiphar's wife. Yet "God's mercy did not delay," as the account says. Evagrius's guardian angel staged an intervention.

One night Evagrius had a vision of shining angels who came to arrest him and take him away. One angel suddenly assumed the likeness of a friend and told him that he was in grave danger and needed to flee the city, adding that if Evagrius promised, then he would assist him. Evagrius swore, woke to pack his bags, and sailed immediately from the city.[46] When it came to his battles with lust, Evagrius was not yet out of the woods. But because his angel came to his aid, he survived to fight another day.

Other times our angels comfort us *after* the trials and temptations we endure. Macarius's cherub, for instance, often came following a demonic attack.[47] That is not to say the angel was absent during the trial, merely that he stood back to allow Macarius to assume his proper station as a follower of Christ—that is, someone who fights the demons and is victorious over them, just as was Christ. Battling temptation makes us stronger. Were our angels to drop in and relieve us in every fight, we'd never learn to stand, which surely Christ desires for all of us. This is the proper way to imagine demonic attacks on believers: God allows them for our maturity and good, particularly to teach us humility.[48]

The pattern can be seen in the life of Jesus himself. While angels appear to have ministered to Christ *during* his Gethsemane passion, they came *after* his temptation in the wilderness. Chrysostom said Christians can expect the same. By observing Christ, he said, "you also may learn, that after your victories which are copied from [Christ's], angels will receive you also, applauding you, and waiting as guards on you in all things."[49]

7

It is interesting to contemplate the society of angels and how ours intersects with theirs. If, for instance, the angels bring judgment on the nations as we see in Revelation, how do those angels interact with the angels over faithful churches and individuals in those same nations? In some cases guardian angels are charged with protecting God's people in the midst of turmoil while other angels pour out judgment on those around them. At the same time, in some cases we know that God allows his people to suffer through such grave occurrences.

One story of the Persian attack on Jerusalem in the year 614 included monks captured outside the city by the advancing army. Led near the city by their captors, the monks took heart. They could somehow see angels arranged across the ramparts, all with fiery lances and shields. But their confidence melted when they saw another angel descend and direct the defenders to leave their posts: "Depart," he said, according to the monks, "for the Lord has given over this holy city into the hands of the enemy." They gazed with dismay as the angels followed their celestial commander away from the city. "And thereby we knew that our sins exceeded God's grace," they said. God was disciplining the people, and part of that was withdrawing their angels.[50]

Our sins offend our guardian angels. If we are unrepentant, they withdraw from us, perhaps not permanently, but we cannot expect or demand their presence in the midst of our sins. When a person persists in pride, for instance, "the angel of providence, who is near him and stirs in him care for righteousness, withdraws from him," said Isaac the Syrian. The person can, he continued, "wrong this angel."[51] This is a curious point, but one that makes sense when we remember that we have a real relationship with our angels. They are not abstract ideas; they are persons, and persons can be harmed and offended by sin.

Angels are humble and holy and prefer the company of those who are likewise humble and holy. Strengthening the bond between our guardian angels and us requires that we grow in humility and holiness.

Jesus said that in heaven we will be like the angels.

Icon of the archangel Michael from about the year 1000. Demons fall in defeat around him.

He was speaking specifically of marriage, that people will not be given in marriage in heaven. But the early Christians considered this statement to be about their lives generally. More than that, they considered our becoming like angels as the goal of our lives right now. That especially concerns cultivating holiness and obedience. The angels are our models here. "Let us," said Chrysostom, "exemplify the life of angels, the virtue of angels, the conversation of angels."[52]

The obedience of the angels ought to inspire and encourage godly service. Clement of Rome, a contemporary and acquaintance of the apostle Paul, made this connection, saying that God "urges us who believe in him with our entire heart not to be idle or slovenly in every good work." What's more, "[W]e should be submissive to his will." Why? Clement pointed us to the angels, who gather around the heavenly throne to minister to their maker, just as we ought.[53] The point is clear enough: if beings so glorious as angels willingly, gladly bow and serve, lowly creatures such as ourselves cannot reasonably withhold ourselves. That is especially true when considering the most fundamental service—worship.

Our companionship with the angels goes beyond protection. Preached the eighth-century British monk Bede, "It is no secret that angels are frequently present, invisibly, at the side of the elect, in order to defend them from the snares of the cunning enemy and uphold them by the great gift of heavenly desire. . . . Nevertheless," he continued, "we should believe that the angelic spirits are especially present to us when we give ourselves in a special way to divine services."[54] It is to that special presence in worship and prayer that we now turn.

6

Voices Ascending

Joining with Angels in Worship and Prayer

O for a thousand seraph tongues
To bless the incarnate Word!
CHARLES WESLEY

1

"I will acknowledge you, O Lord, with my whole heart," says the psalmist; "before angels I will make music to you."[1] The lyric grabs hold of the mind and opens it to a reality both powerful and humbling: we offer our praise and prayers amid angels and archangels. They surround and even assist us as we press toward the heavenly throne.

God intended us to understand this reality. When he directed Moses to erect the tabernacle, his instructions included weaving ten curtains and a veil of blue, purple, and scarlet thread. God commanded these sheets be embroidered with, among other imagery, cherubim. The ark of the covenant was similarly decorated with twin cherubim of gold, statues fixed on either side of the ark's lid, the mercy seat. The tabernacle was the center of worship, and the ark was the center of the center, in the Holy of Holies, upon which Moses and the high priest heard God speak.[2]

The cherubim retained their place when King Solomon later built the temple. As detailed in the sixth, seventh, and eighth chapters of I Kings, the craftsmen carved cherubim in olivewood, covered them in gold for the doors, and placed them all over the walls. Solomon additionally had two massive olivewood cherub statues created, each ten feet high with ten-foot wingspans. He covered them with gold and placed them in the inner sanctum, outstretched over the ark in the Holy of Holies.

A mosaic in the apse of the church of Germigny-des-Prés in Orleans, France, shows what's going on. The ark is depicted with its golden-sculpted cherubim upon the lid, but there, standing to the side are two huge living cherubim, wings outstretched, each extending hands in the sign of blessing. The mosaic is telling us that the sculpture assumes the reality.[3]

Christians have always believed this. Paul said in Hebrews that the old covenant temple was patterned on the heavenly temple, a "copy and shadow of the heavenly sanctuary."[4] He also said that God gave the old covenant as a "tutor."[5] The prophet and the king placed cherubic images in the place of worship to depict and declare the unseen reality, that living cherubim also populate the place of worship. The icons were meant as windows to heaven, and the Israelites were disciples to the teaching that they worship with and among heavenly hosts, each and all offering hymns and prayers to their Creator and Redeemer.

Paul pulled back the curtain for us. "[Y]ou have come to Mount Zion and to the city of the living God, the heavenly Jerusalem," as he said in Hebrews, "and to innumerable angels in festal gathering."[6] The prophets Micaiah, Isaiah, and Daniel had seen this reality; Paul as well. So did Paul's contemporary, the apostle John.

2

One of the most enigmatic books of Scripture is the book of Revelation, also known as the Apocalypse of John. It vividly and violently portrays the struggle of the church in the world at the end of the age. John opened by saying that the "revelation" was given to him by an angel of God. He additionally prefaced the work by saying, "I was in the Spirit on the Lord's day"—a significant statement that contextualizes much of what follows.[7]

Sunday is the Lord's Day, the day on which Christians gather to pray and worship, offer the liturgy, and celebrate the victory of Christ over sin, death, and the Devil through the resurrection. As the vision unfurled, John found himself mystically present in the midst of a heavenly worship service, Paul's "festal gathering." Wrote John,

> I looked, and lo, in heaven an open door! . . . At once
> I was in the Spirit, and lo, a throne stood in heaven,
> with one seated on the throne! . . . From the throne
> issue flashes of lightning, and voices and peals of
> thunder, and before the throne burn seven torches of
> fire, which are the seven spirits of God.[8]

First depicted in Revelation as lampstands, these seven spirits are angels who stand at the foot of God's throne.[9] The book of Tobit, in which the archangel Raphael plays a major role, offers the first glimpse of these seven spirits. Near the end of the story Raphael announces himself as "one of the seven holy angels who present the prayers of the saints and enter into the presence of the glory of the Holy One."[10] As mentioned in chapter 4, the archangel Gabriel also identifies himself as one of these seven angels who stand in the presence.[11]

This is where John stood, in the glorious presence of God. Around him were "many angels, numbering myriads of myriads and thousands of thousands."[12] Cherubim sang, "Holy, holy, holy, is the Lord God Almighty, who was and is and is to come!" and offered incense and prayers, all before the Lamb opened the scroll and read the Word.[13]

The intrigue of John's vision is that earthly liturgies we offer each Lord's Day are a part of a wider, ever-occurring angelic worship service. That's what Moses was telling us through the tabernacle decoration and what Paul was saying explicitly in Hebrews. When we come before the Lord in worship, we are coming mid-service. Already arrayed are countless angels and the departed faithful, praising and hymning the Creator. John saw in vivid color what most Christians experience in shades, but we should see it nonetheless. The liturgy elevates us to the throne of God where we join our angelic siblings in worship and prayer.

It's for this reason that, like Moses and Solomon first, the ancient Christians frequently insisted on adorning their churches with painted frescoes, tile mosaics, and other icons of the angels who are present and praising with us. Like the images, the ancient liturgies of the church affirm the same point, in their own way echoing what Paul and John experienced and declared. As the church comes together, its members self-consciously gather with the angels around the altar of God.

The church borrowed the term *liturgy* from secular life. The Greek word *leitourgia* implies a public-works project, a collective labor. It turns out to be a very fitting loan word because in the city of God, worship is the work of the inhabitants, both visible and invisible.

3

During the entrance of the priest into the sanctuary in *The Divine Liturgy of James*, the deacon prays, "The Lord bless us, and make us worthy [like the seraphim] to offer gifts, and to sing the oft-sung hymn of the divine trisagion," otherwise known as the thrice-holy hymn. It is the seraphim who sing, "Holy, holy, holy," and tradition suggests that angels taught humans the trisagion ("Holy God, Holy Mighty, Holy Immortal, have mercy on us"), something we'll explore later in this chapter.[14] Suffice it to say for now, we sing, as the *James* liturgy puts it, "together with the heavenly powers."[15]

The liturgy further informs us that those heavenly powers include "angels, archangels, thrones, dominions, principalities, and authorities, and dread powers; and the many-eyed cherubim, and the six-winged seraphim . . . crying one to another with unresting lips, with unceasing praises."[16]

Another early liturgy, *The Liturgy of the Blessed Apostles*, restates the thought:

Thy majesty, O Lord, thousands of thousands of heavenly spirits, and ten thousand myriads of holy angels, hosts of spirits, ministers of fire and spirit, bless and adore; with the holy cherubim and the spiritual seraphim they sanctify and celebrate Thy name, crying and praising, without ceasing unto each other.[17]

All the various versions of the divine liturgy feature psalms, hymns, and Scripture readings, but the central act is the Eucharist, the moment that the church on earth commemorates and participates in the eternal, once-and-for-all sacrifice of Christ. The church on earth is not alone. "We are not permitted to doubt that where the mysteries of the Lord's body and blood are being enacted, a gathering of citizens from on high is present," said Bede. To drive home the point, Bede added that these were, after all, the same beings who kept such careful watch over Christ's tomb before his resurrection.[18] Their absence from the offering is unthinkable.

As we offer the bread and wine, the church represents in some mystical sense these angelic participants. The hymn writers of the church draw our attention to the fact. Since the sixth century, churches have sung the Cherubikon, or the "Cherubic Hymn," as the priest and deacons process around the congregation and toward the altar with the gifts of bread and wine:

Let us who mystically portray the Cherubim, and chant the thrice-holy hymn unto the life-creating

Trinity, lay aside all earthly care; that we may receive the King of all, escorted invisibly by the Angelic orders. Alleluia, alleluia, alleluia.[19]

This version of the hymn seems to condense an earlier one. Here it is more elaborately from *The Divine Liturgy of James*:

Let all mortal flesh be silent, and stand with fear and trembling, and meditate nothing earthly within itself:

For the King of kings and Lord of lords, Christ our God, comes forward to be sacrificed and to be given for food to the faithful; and the bands of angels go before Him with every power and domin- ion, the many-eyed cherubim, and the six-winged seraphim, covering their faces and crying aloud the hymn, Alleluia, Alleluia, Alleluia.[20]

On earth the image is humble, a few priests and dea- cons, some acolytes, moving in uneven procession. But the liturgies encourage us to grasp a fuller reality, even a truer reality. The procession is thick with worshippers, a long train of celestial attendants. These angels stand with men as we mutually serve the King. "Now the hosts of Heaven invisibly worship with us," says one liturgy; "for behold, the King of Glory doth enter. Behold, the accomplished mystical Sacrifice is being escorted."[21]

VOICES ASCENDING

Worshippers mention the angels in their prayers and hymns as a way of mutual participation, "so we may be partakers with the hosts of the world above in their hymn of praise," as Cyril of Jerusalem said in his *Catechetical Lectures*.[22] Though there seems to be a great divide between heaven and earth, our worlds overlap and interlock, and nothing draws them closer together than worship. "[O]ur things are in heaven," said John Chrysostom, "and heavenly things are ours, even though they be accomplished on earth."[23]

4

As the service continues, the gifts are placed upon the altar, and we see the angels pressing in, crowding around. "[A]ngels stand by the priest," said John Chrysostom; "and the whole sanctuary, and the space round about the altar, is filled with the powers of heaven, in honor of Him who lies thereon," by whom he meant Christ.[24]

The priest offers up the gifts, and the Holy Spirit descends upon them in power, mystically transforming the bread and wine. As he does so, said Symeon d-Taibutha in *The Book of Grace*, an ancient monastic text from Syria, "The cherubim, the seraphim, and the angels stand with great awe, fear, and joy. They rejoice over the Holy Mysteries while experiencing inexpressible astonishment."[25]

The priest's prayers assume this busy scene. Read this from *The Divine Liturgy of the Holy Apostle and Evangelist Mark*: "We pray and beseech, Thee, O Lord, in Thy mercy, to let Thy presence rest upon this bread and these chalices on the all-holy table, while angels, archangels, and Thy holy priests stand round and minister for Thy glory and the renewing of our souls."[26]

In his book *On the Priesthood*, Chrysostom related the story of a "venerable man, accustomed to see revelations" and described how once during the Eucharist, he suddenly saw "so far as was possible for him, a multitude of angels, clothed in shining robes, and encircling the altar, and bending down, as one might see soldiers in the presence of their King, and for my part," said Chrysostom, "I believe it."[27] Others have seen such visions as well. "Not a Saturday or a Sunday passed," monastic father Macarius of Alexandria told one of his disciples, "that I did not see the angel of the altar standing in front of me as I celebrated the Holy Communion of God."[28]

The same Macarius observed the following about Mark the Monk, a monastic writer we quoted earlier and who lived in Macarius's community: "I saw at the time of the mysteries that I did not give the sacrament to Mark the Ascetic a single time but when he came to receive communion I would see an angel placing the sacrament in his hands." In one version of the story, Macarius added that he only saw the angel's hands administer the sacrament.[29]

As with so much of Christian belief and practice, angels delivering the elements of Communion are foreshadowed in the Old Testament. Recall from the story of Daniel and Habakkuk. An angel scooped up the latter by the hair to deliver a meal to Daniel, then in the lions' den. Although the story is missing from many Bibles today, the early Christians read and valued it because of its allusions to the Eucharist. One illustration of the event, carved on a sarcophagus, depicts the loaf in Habakkuk's basket as marked with a cross, an anachronistic allusion to Eucharistic bread.[30] And the Old Greek version of the Septuagint adds a telling detail to the story. Habakkuk brings not only bread in this version but also a flagon of wine, a Eucharistic detail also captured by religious artists.[31] Carving the image on a sarcophagus possibly served as a statement that victory over death comes only from communion with Christ.

5

For the Christian the sacrament is sustenance and ultimately the greatest satisfaction. Christians participate in the life of God through Communion, just as angels do directly. Augustine explained this thought by elaborating upon the intriguing phrase "bread of angels."

The phrase first appears in Psalm 78 where it refers to manna, something I mentioned here in chapter 3.

God sent "the grain of heaven," said the psalmist. "Man ate of the bread of the angels; he sent them food in abundance."[32] The Wisdom of Solomon later echoes, "[T]hou didst give thy people food of angels, and without their toil thou didst supply them from heaven with bread," adding a sacramental nuance in saying that the bread "was changed" according "to the desire of the one who took it."[33]

Here's what Augustine did with it. In commenting on Psalm 78, the great bishop and exegete said that Christ is the "true Bread from Heaven" and "indeed the food of angels, whom being incorruptible the Word of God doth incorruptibly feed."[34] The angels take their sustenance from the one who gave them substance. They feast on the very presence and power of God or, as he said later in the same book, the "truth" and "goodness of God," the goodness out of whose overflow they were created in the first place.[35] Echoed John Damascene, "They behold God . . . and this is their food."[36]

What of us humans? After all, Augustine said that we and the angels "live not on different meat."[37] But we are not incorruptible like our spiritual siblings. For us to take sustenance from the presence of God, the presence must become palpable. Man's life comes not from material bread alone, as Christ said, but from the word of God.[38] How do we access that word? It's not just by listening to Scriptures and soliloquies, though that's important. Nor is it merely hearing the hymns and homilies, though those are helpful too.

The sixth chapter of John's gospel paints a difficult picture for some, but in it Christ points back to the Psalter and the Wisdom of Solomon and identifies himself with the bread from heaven. "I am the living bread which came down from heaven," he said, "and the bread which I shall give for the life of the world is my flesh. . . . [U]nless you eat the flesh of the Son of man and drink his blood, you have no life in you; he who eats my flesh and drinks my blood has eternal life."[39]

It's a shocking set of verses, but the very thing that makes it scandalous, its physicality, offers us the key to understanding it. For Augustine, it was the incarnation that unlocked the mystery. "That man might eat angels' food," he said, "the Creator of the angels was made man."[40] How do humans live by the truth of God? How do we ingest and gain sustenance from the goodness of God? Through the incarnate person of Christ, in whose life we participate by the sacrament of Communion. We take wine and bread, mystically change them by God's power and our desire, and sup with angels.

It won't always be like this, said Augustine. Talking about the Lord's Prayer, he identified the Eucharist with "our daily bread," as do most ancient commentators. He added to the Eucharist the services of the church, the Scripture readings, and hymns and said, "[T]hese are necessary in our state of pilgrimage." But what about when we get to heaven? "Do the angels need books, and interpreters, and readers? Surely not," he said. "They read in seeing, for the Truth Itself they see, and are abundantly satisfied from that fountain, from which we obtain some few drops." It will be the same with us. When we pass into eternity, we "shall see the Word Himself, and hear the Word Himself, and eat and drink Him as the angels do now."[41] The Scriptures, the liturgy, the Eucharist— these are gracious condescensions for our creaturehood. And their very grace and condescension evoke worship. "If you taste," said Augustine, "sing praises; if ye have tasted how sweet the Lord is, sing praises."[42]

Given the sustenance supplied by the bread of angels, it should not surprise us that our guardian angels are saddened and even "made indignant" when we willingly deprive ourselves of Communion, as Symeon d-Taibutha said in *The Book of Grace*. But when each of us participates, "The angel who is always by us is consoled, because he also partakes."[43]

These ancient rites—still practiced by the faithful today—assume the reality of Isaiah's vision, of Daniel's vision, of John's vision. By faith, believers join the angels in our common labor, the worship of God. But there is still more mutual involvement in our heavenly approach.

6

Go back to Augustine's crowded urban streets. We live in a larger city, one where angels and people rub shoulders.

While we feel alone, sometimes horribly alone, we nonetheless stand and pray amid a host of angels. If we could pull the veil, we would see them watching, suggesting, participating, sharing, and interceding.

In *The Ladder of Divine Ascent*, John Climacus called prayer the "work of angels."[44] And readers of the Scripture and other ancient Christian texts cannot fail to notice that the angels are not shirkers.

The archangels Gabriel and Raphael, as we saw earlier, identify themselves as angels who stand in the presence of God. Raphael's explanation includes the detail that the purpose of this position is to hear and bring prayers before God. He says that he "present[s] the prayers of the saints" and that he "brought a reminder of your prayer before the Holy One."[45] Gabriel's task is the same, as we see in the book of Daniel, shuttling messages to and fro. The role is evident enough in the tradition that in his disquisition on prayer, fourth-century writer Aphrahat the Persian referred several times to Gabriel as "the angel who offers prayers."[46]

It is not just archangels like Gabriel and Raphael who offer prayers. All angels, including our guardian angels, relay our prayers and plights to God. As we've already seen, angels represent us and advocate for us in heaven. John's vision in Revelation provides us pictures of angels offering prayers. We earlier referenced one such scene. Look here at another:

And another angel came and stood at the altar with a golden censer; and he was given much incense to mingle with the prayers of all the saints upon the golden altar before the throne; and the smoke of the incense rose with the prayers of the saints from the hand of the angel before God.[47]

Some may bristle at the thought of prayers going through intermediaries. I think the objection mirrors the objection that some have when hearing that angels mediate divine encounters, as happens so often in the Old Testament. If so, it's a misplaced objection. To say that angels offer our prayers to God does not mean that God fails to hear our prayers directly. Isaac the Syrian said that the eternal will of God "anticipates prayer."[48] Our prayers are in the mind of God before we even conceive them. He is not waiting for a message to cross the transom. Our thoughts, said Clement of Alexandria, cut right through air and the whole material world in an instant.[49] And as Jacob of Serugh put it, "[N]o angel is as swift-winged as prayer [itself]."[50]

Nevertheless, God chooses to use means, and so the angels have an intermediary, intercessory role in our lives. In a sense this is no different than saying God takes care of our needs via our salaries or the charity of neighbors, or saying that God rules the earth via earthly governors. He is no less involved for their greater involvement; they are simply part of the way that he is involved. In the same way, God has appointed angels to work our prayers. And there are reasons to be grateful about this fact.

The apostle John watches as seven angels trumpet and one stands before an altar and loads a censer with incense, representing prayers. The image is a medieval manuscript illumination from the Bamberg Apocalypse.

Aside from the vivid image of an angel presenting our prayers to God, it is intriguing to contemplate the fact that our angels add to our prayers, as we see in the just-quoted passage from Revelation. He is given extra incense to offer with the petitions, amplifying our prayers with prayers of his own. And there's more. Besides enhancing our prayers, the angels make our concerns their own, as Raphael does. Recall that he "reminds" God of people's prayers. He wants to ensure that God is aware of their need, and he takes responsibility for the cares of the people to whom he is assigned.

The early church certainly understood things this way, and you can thus find many references to the efficacious prayers of the angels in the theological, mystical, and pastoral writings. Ambrose of Milan, for instance, urged that we prayerfully invoke not only the saints and martyrs but also the angels: "The angels must be entreated for us, who have been to us as guards," he said.[51] The ancients also counseled caution about praying to angels as gods or worshipping them.[52] But properly bounded, a relationship with one's angel is normal, particularly around prayer.

7

If prayer is the "work of angels" as John Climacus said, then as humans we are privileged to join the labor. But the early writers were quick to caution us. There is tremendous gravity inherent to the task, requiring that we be mindful as we, in Augustine's words, "knock at the ears of God by prayer."[53]

Sometimes we knock just as we wake in the morning; other times in the thick of a busy day or during the drowsy moments before sleep. But in all settings, the ancient preachers and theologians of the church advised and even demanded watchfulness. In one of his homilies on Hebrews, John Chrysostom offered the picture of a man approaching God as he was "gaping and scratching himself," while the angels "[stood] by in fear and trembling."[54] The fourth-century monastic Evagrius was less glib. "Arouse yourself, wretch; your Lord is speaking with you," he said, apparently unworried about offending his listeners. "Do not wander off. His elect angels surround you, do not be dismayed; the ranks of the demons stand facing you, so do not grow lax."[55]

As the ancient Christians understood things, prayer is serious work and requires sober-minded practitioners. The angelic presence around us ought to encourage and engender watchfulness.

The angelic presence should also encourage and engender a desire to pray. When evil spirits come close, we feel uneasy and afraid; but when we sense the presence of a guardian angel, we feel at ease, humble, and joyful. Climacus said the very feeling can alert us to the angelic presence, and when it does, he urged us to "hasten to prayer, for our good guardian has come to pray with us."[56] As we pray, our awareness of the angel's presence may grow. "If you feel sweetness or compunction at some word of your prayer, dwell on it," he said, "for then our guardian angel is praying with us."[57]

Knowing to *whom* and with *whom* we pray should inform for *what* we pray. As the Cherubikon encourages us to dispense with earthly cares, so the subject of our prayers should be elevated as well—without frivolous and base requests. Isaac the Syrian said that when we ask for earthly things, it's like a subject standing before his king and imploring him for a measure of manure. The request insults both the king and the subject. As if to make the embarrassment all the more apparent, Isaac reminded us that "the King's great officials, [angels and archangels,] are gazing steadfastly upon you at the time of your prayer to see what petition you will make of their Master; and they are astonished and exultant whenever they behold one who is made of earth forsake his dunghill and ask for what is heavenly."[58]

In some cases the angels reject our prayers. Aphrahat said that when we pray while bearing a grudge or ill will against our neighbor, we offer an impure offering. "Gabriel, who presents prayers," he said, "does not want to take it from earth because, on inspection, he has found a blemish in your offering."[59] Before he will offer our prayer in the censer before God's throne, Gabriel insists we make good with our neighbor and offer a pure prayer.[60]

The management or oversight aspect of the angels' role manifests in other ways, including instructing people how to pray. One example: we should offer our thanksgiving to God first, next confessions of sin, and only then should we request anything of God. "This," said John Climacus, "is the best way of prayer, as it is shown to one of the brethren by an angel of the Lord."[61] It was likewise from an angel that the monastic father Pachomius the Great learned the daily prayer rule that he and his fellow monks followed.[62]

According to tradition, even the Trisagion itself was taught by angels. The Trisagion is one of the most cherished and constantly used prayers in the church: "Holy God, Holy Mighty, Holy Immortal, have mercy on us." The seraphim sang a version of this in Isaiah's vision of heaven, and angels taught it to us on earth. In the middle of the fifth century, a series of terrible earthquakes shook the region around Constantinople. Tremors brought down homes and reduced great buildings to ruin. As aftershocks continued, Archbishop Proclus gathered his people to pray for deliverance. Suddenly, from the midst of the congregation, angels snatched a boy out of sight. When he returned some moments later, the boy recited the Trisagion just as the angels had taught him. The people followed suit, called out, and the quakes ceased.[63]

8

Because of the power of prayer and its function of draw-ing us closer to God, the demons are anxious to foul our efforts. They conjure distraction, worry, and fear in our minds. John Climacus, for instance, wrote about the demon of grief that "tries to devastate our prayer" by making our sins seem great and God distant.[64] Another writer, Martyrius, related how Satan tries to bring slum-ber to our minds and eyes when he sees us "keeping vigil with our Lord . . . exhibiting the wakefulness of the angels" in our prayer.[65]

According to Climacus, our prayers are followed by "swarms of demons" who attempt to steal our spiritual gains. If we stay the course, their attacks will amount to nothing. As believers press through the difficulties and grow in prayer, we find "the unholy spirits . . . flee as from fire when scourged by prayer."[66]

In the meantime, as we await our ultimate victory, we offer praise and pray with the angels, who, in Climacus's words, "unite in worship with him whose soul is quiet, and dwell lovingly with him."[67]

Final Companions

Guides from One World to the Next

O bear me, ye cherubim, up,
And waft me away to his throne.
WILLIAM COWPER, *Olney Hymns*

1

Moses was very old when he died, one hundred and twenty years. The final chapter of Deuteronomy says that he was physically strong, that his eyes were undimmed, and that no one was so great a prophet as he. Following his death, Satan and Michael argued over his body. The only place Scripture mentions the contest is in the short epistle of Jude, and there only in passing. As the account goes, the Devil came to claim the prophet's corpse, but Michael rebuked him and kept safe the body.[1]

The picture is simultaneously disturbing and comforting. Disturbing because it shows Satan taking interest in the Lord's departed, looking at the saints as contested property, as prizes to be seized. But it's strangely comforting because the story also shows us that the angels are with us through death and guard us even then. And not just our bodies, but our souls especially.

"[T]o be absent from the body," Paul wrote the church at Corinth, is "to be present with the Lord."[2] But it's not necessarily an instantaneous transition. Scripture and the ancient Christian writers invite us to contemplate angels as escorts who guide us through the passage of death to take us to the side of Christ.

2

In Luke's gospel, Jesus told the story of a rich man and Lazarus. The rich man was decked in fine attire and served the most sumptuous foods, while Lazarus the beggar sat sickly and starving by the rich man's door, dogs licking his open wounds. When Lazarus died, according to Jesus, he "was carried by the angels to Abraham's bosom," a poetic reference to the place where the righteous went when they died.[3] These angels, said Asterius of Amasea, "were his body-guard, looking upon him gently and mildly, and betokening by their manner the attendance and relief that awaited him."[4]

In his *Ecclesiastical History*, Bede recounted the passing of a beloved nun named Earcongota. She was a godly and gracious woman, loved by the whole community. Before her death she received intimation that her end was soon coming. She saw a vision of white-robed men entering the monastery, looking for her. Said Bede, "And on the very night when, as dawn drew near, she left the darkness of this world and entered the light of heaven, many brethren of the monastery, who lived in separate buildings, said that they had clearly heard choirs of angels singing and a sound like that of a great throng entering the monastery." The monks ran out to investigate and "saw a great light coming down from heaven, which carried away the holy soul of Earcongota."[5] Of the many times that Bede mentioned angels in his *Ecclesiastical History*, most all involve spiritual escorts like Earcongota's.

Death can be frightening, but we should take heart that angels guard us on the journey. Bede told the story of an Irish monk named Fursey. Carried aloft by angels in a vision, Fursey came upon a roaring aerial conflagration, through which he and the angels had to pass—understandably to Fursey's great alarm. To clear a path, one angel rushed ahead and divided the flame like the waters of the Red Sea, carving a path through which Fursey could pass.[6]

Chrysostom related something similar. Recalling the three youths protected by an angel in the Babylonian fire, Chrysostom said that at death, "saints walking through the river of fire shall suffer no pain, nay they will even appear joyous." Not so for the wicked. For those who bow the knee to the idols of the world, there are "flame and torment," said Chrysostom. On that side "stands the devil," but for those who bow the knee only to Christ, there are "dew and refreshment" and "angels wafting aside the flame."[7] When I contemplate the scene, I imagine the rush of the angels' wings keeping flames at bay as we pass with ease to the bosom of Christ.

The psalmist said that the death of the saints is precious in God's eyes.[8] We can only imagine that the angels, whose very mission is to bring us to and through a saving experience of Christ, agree. Not only is our death the end of our journey here; it's the final milestone in their service.

When believers take last rites, according to Chrysostom, the angels press around: "[I]f they happen to be partakers of the mysteries, with a pure conscience, when they are about to breathe their last, angels keep guard over them for the sake of what they have received, and bear them hence." Chrysostom claimed to know someone who had mystically seen and heard it happen once.[9]

Iconographic depictions sometimes show angels stooping over the body of a dead saint, their hands respectfully wrapped in their cloaks, ready to receive the soul of the deceased.[10]

While praying, the fourth-century ascetic bishop Nephon experienced a vision in which he saw angels from heaven "ascend[ing] and descend[ing] like bees, transporting the souls of people who had died." In several instances demons stopped the traffic and claimed the heaven-bound soul as rightly their own. The person died in his sins, the demons would say. But the angels would contend for their charges, appealing to the mercy and grace of God and arguing for the person's repentance against the lies of the demons. In part of the vision that aligns with the story of Michael and the body of Moses, Nephon saw an angel called from his place of guarding the body of his recently deceased charge. Later he saw a godly woman welcomed to heaven by angels "embracing and kissing her tenderly." As they gathered around her they sang, "Glory to God Who delivered this soul from the dreadful dragon!"[11]

The angels rejoiced when God entered our world, and they rejoice again when we enter his. Because our final success is their success, it's appropriate to contemplate the angels rejoicing at our homecoming. In a eulogy for Acholius, the bishop of Thessalonica, Ambrose of Milan expressed regret that this "veteran . . . of Christ" had departed life on this earth, but "freed from the bands of the body," he was "carried by the ministry of angels to the intimate presence of Christ." While Acholius left grievers here on earth, the angels met him with "jubilation," rejoicing "that such a man had come among them."[12]

What a great source of comfort to think of death not as cold passage but one conducted by angels whose arms shelter and protect as they carry us, finally reunited, to the throne of God, and one all the more wonderful to imagine when considering their joy in the service. How must they look upon us, so worthy and tender in their eyes.

3

Angels escort us individually to the throne of grace, and they are involved in a more collective endeavor. Jesus spoke of the angels coming with him at the end. The angels will appear at a trumpet's blast and gather God's people "from the four winds, from one end of heaven to the other." When this day will arrive, no one knows, not even the angels, but they will have an active and decisive part to play.[13]

Jesus gave us the picture of a harvest and the angels as reapers. When the harvest is at last ripe, the angels are charged with separating the wheat from the weeds, the children of God from the followers of the Devil. "The angels will come out and separate the evil from the righteous," said Jesus, adding the ominous warning, "and throw them [the evil] into the furnace of fire." This fire, we are told elsewhere, was "prepared for the devil and his angels" but will torment those who refused to serve

Christ.[14] Paul painted the same image in his letters to the Thessalonians.[15]

Those who love and confess Christ, Christ loves and confesses before God and the angels; but those who are ashamed of him or turn their backs, Christ denies before God and the angels. Angels serve in this regard as witnesses to our lives, something Paul indicated, validating the judgments of God.[16] Could it be that the Old Testament law demanding that facts be established by two or more witnesses reflects this deep-seated order in the cosmos, a primary function of the angels in whose presence we live out our lives? Recall that the sins of Sodom and Gomorrah were known to God and validated by his angels. They testify to our good and also to our evil, for they, like God, have seen it all. They are "watchers" in more than name.

This judgment is part of Christ repaying us according to our deeds, which he affirms he will do at the end.[17] Scripture uses the pastoral image of the shepherd separating sheep and goats. A sixth-century mosaic in the Basilica of Sant'Apollinare Nuovo in Ravenna, Italy, captures the scene with sheep on Christ's right hand and goats on his left. By the sheep stands a red angel, the color indicating his reflection of God's uncreated light; by the goats stands a blue angel, the Devil, as indicated by his cool hue, one that long since stopped reflecting the light of the Lord.[18]

This great judgment includes not only us but also

the angels. "Let no one be deceived," Ignatius reminded the Smyrneans. "Judgment is prepared even for the heavenly beings, for the glory of the angels, and for the rulers both visible and invisible."[19] Those angels that stayed loyal to their Creator will rejoice, while those that turned with Satan and worked evil will be judged and even tormented in the fire prepared for them.

Amazingly, Paul told the Corinthians that Christians will participate in judging the world and that we will join the judgment of angels.[20] Theodoret of Cyrus commented, "By angels he means demons, for they were angels once upon a time." For what could we judge them? Theodoret speculated, "The saints will condemn them because, though clad in a body, they had care for the divine liturgy, whereas those creatures, though naturally bodiless, adopted evil ways."[21] In other words, whereas people have the distractions from worship and obedience that come with physicality and bodily passions, such as weariness, lust, and hunger, the angels have no such impediments.

4

Our participation in judging the angels is one aspect of a great reversal, the lesser beings holding court over the greater. But the greater reversal is the one at the very root of reality when God reveals the remedy to all ills.

Driven by envy and malice, Satan means to do nothing but evil, but being love and mercy, God turns the Devil's handiwork to good. Since God foreknows everything, he was fully aware from the beginning that man would fall away. But as all thought is simultaneous in God, he "also knew what good . . . he would bring out of man's evil," as Augustine said.[22] This counts not only for the evil that men do, but also for the foundational act of evil that preceded all other acts of evil.

None of it caught God by surprise. Less did it dissuade him from creating all the worlds from the overflow of his goodness. Every evil that Satan would work was matched in the mind of God with its remedy. No evil occurs without a greater good already bursting into existence. Satan, as C. S. Lewis memorably said, "is allowed to do all the evil he wants and finds that he has produced good."[23]

In the first of three homilies concerning demons, Chrysostom argued that God allows the Devil to inflict evil on us the same way a parent chastens a child. When God allows the demons room to harass us, he is not deserting us. He desires, said Chrysostom, "to crown [us], and make [us] more distinguished." If we endure, we grow in grace. If we endure to the end, we will be rewarded just as Job was.[24]

This is the staggering asymmetry of God's goodness. There is more grace than envy, more love than hate, more heaven than hell.[25]

5

We dwell in a great and sprawling city, one in which we live and serve alongside angels. For all but a few, this reality is dim at best. Most wander through life unaware of their spiritual surroundings and their angelic neighbors. Some have been granted extraordinary visions of this dimension, and they peer with unhindered eyes and hearts at our celestial siblings, these elder brothers who labor to bring us up, to aid us, to draw us to the bosom of Christ. Would that we could be just as aware even if we never see such radiance until the moment the angels come to take us.

We began this meditation with the words of Augustine, and it's fitting to close with them as well. Recollecting the death of Cyprian of Carthage, Augustine comforted and encouraged his congregation:

> [W]hen our mourning shall have passed away, we all with one voice, in one people, in one country, shall receive comfort, thousands of thousands joined with angels playing upon harps, with choirs of heavenly powers *living in one city*.[26]

Notes

I have quoted the Old Testament from the Septuagint in several instances, particularly when a certain point was more clearly evident in the Septuagint or when it reflected more closely the apparent view of the ancient church. I've indicated reliance and particular translation by flagging citations either NETS or HTM. In some cases this reliance can cause confusion because of certain differences between the Septuagint and the Masoretic text (from which we get most of our modern English Bibles). This is especially so in the Psalter, in which chapter and verse numbers vary somewhat; to help mitigate misunderstanding, I default to the Masoretic numbering except when quoting from the Septuagint, in which case I use the Septuagint numbering and place the Masoretic in parentheses.

Regarding the work of ancient Christian sources, since many of the translations quoted throughout the book are quite old, I've taken the liberty of minimally updating the material wherever it seemed appropriate and helpful, especially as to what a modern eye might consider an overreliance on capitalization.

CHAPTER 1. OUR LARGER CITY

1. For purposes of this book, I'm defining "ancient church" roughly as the first seven centuries after Christ, though the iconography mentioned and featured will include several later but illustrative examples.
2. Acts 23.8.
3. Augustine, *City of God* 12.1.
4. Hebrews 1.14. Though his authorship is contested by some, Paul is traditionally assumed to have written Hebrews. I follow that assumption here.
5. Augustine, *City of God* 12.1.
6. Augustine, *On Christian Doctrine* 1.30.
7. Augustine, *Homilies on the Gospel of John* 107.2.
8. Gregory of Nyssa also stressed this celestial fraternity, comparing angels' service to Aaron's help of his brother, Moses. *The Life of Moses* 2.43, 47, 51.
9. Genesis 3.24.
10. Psalm 104.4 NKJV.
11. See note 45 below.
12. Genesis 3.1–5.
13. Gregory Nazianzen, *Orations* 38.9.
14. John Damascene, *Exposition* 2.2.
15. Augustine, *Handbook* 59.
16. Augustine, *City of God* 11.32.

17. Basil, *Hexaemeron* 2.3.

18. Ibid. 1.5. Along with *The Hexaemeron*, see section 38 in Basil's *On the Holy Spirit*, which says in part, "The written account of the origin of the world revealed to us the creation of the heavenly powers only from what is perceptible, and so the manner of their creation is left in silence. But you have the power to reason from the seen to the unseen, and you glorify the Maker in whom all things were created." While Basil and others, like his close friend Gregory Nazianzen, seemed to think that the angels were created before the physical world, following this tack of reasoning from seen to unseen would also permit thinking of their creation as simultaneous with our own, as Augustine thought. Augustine mentioned Basil's view in *City of God* and said a believer is safe holding either view, as they are both edifying (11.32).

19. Revelation 19.17; 9.1; 12.4.

20. Judges 5.20, 23.

21. Job 38.7.

22. Augustine, *Handbook* 58.

23. Augustine, *City of God* 11.9. Augustine commented at length on the angelic light as divine contemplation and knowledge in *The Literal Meaning of Genesis* (e.g., 1.3; 2.8; 4.22, 24, 29–32). The pseudepigraphal *Book of Jubilees*, written sometime in the second century before Christ, also reflects the view that angels were created on the first day: "For on the first day He created the heavens which are above and the earth and the waters and all the spirits which serve before him" (2.2).

24. Isaac the Syrian, *Ascetical Homilies* 26.

25. Marco Bussagli, *Angels*, trans. Rosanna M. Giammanco Frongia (New York: Abrams, 2007), 16, 96.

26. John Damascene, *Exposition* 2.3.

27. James 1.17.

28. Gregory Nazianzen, *Orations* 38.10.

29. Job 38.4–7.

30. Gregory Nazianzen, "Concerning Spiritual Beings," line 14.

31. Basil, *On the Holy Spirit* 38.

32. Psalm 104.4; Judges 13.20; Ezekiel 8.2; Daniel 10.6. Revelation 10.1 similarly describes an angel "wrapped in a cloud, with a rainbow over his head, and his face was like the sun, and his legs like pillars of fire."

33. John Damascene, *Exposition* 2.3.

34. Revelation 21.17. In his book *Jacob's Ladder* (Grand Rapids: Eerdmans, 2010) twentieth-century Russian theologian Sergius Bulgakov extensively developed the idea of the human-angelic relationship by contemplating this verse.

35. See, for instance, *Abraham's Hospitality, Jacob's Ladder*, and *Balaam's Ass*, in Bussagli, *Angels*, 124, 172, 210.

36. Jerome, *Apology* 1.23.

37. John Damascene, *Exposition* 2.3.

38. Regarding the various biblical designations of angels, see Ezekiel 10.14–16, 20; Isaiah 6.2; Ephesians 1.21; Colossians 1.16; 1 Thessalonians 4.16; and Jude 9.

39. Zechariah 2.3; Daniel 10.13.

40. Augustine, *Handbook* 58; Cyril of Jerusalem, *Catechetical Lectures* 11.12.

41. The root, *saraph*, according to the classic Brown, Driver, Briggs, Gesenius Lexicon, means "to burn"; interestingly, the word also means "fiery serpent."

42. Isaiah 6.2.

43. See, for example, Bussagli, *Angels*, 380–84; Alfredo Tradigo, *Icons and Saints of the Eastern Orthodox Church*, trans.

Stephen Sartarelli (Los Angeles: J. Paul Getty Museum, 2006), 56–58.

44. Psalm 18.10.

45. Detailed descriptions of cherubim can be found in Ezekiel 1.5–14; 10.14–16, 20; and Revelation 4.6–8.

 While the ancient Jews also depicted the cherubim in the tabernacle and temple, in his *Antiquities*, Josephus noted that the style of their representations has been lost, so we do not know how they were depicted (8.3).

 The cuddly cupids so often called cherubs from Renaissance and Baroque art are in fact Italian *putti*, a holdover from classical paganism. As to the less cuddly, the gryphon to which the cherubim are often linked is one of many mythic human-animal compounds and comes in different forms, including the Babylonian *lamassu*—which has a man's head, bull's body, and eagle's wings—upon which gods were said to ride.

 The connection between gryphons and cherubim has led many to assume that the ancient Jews borrowed the concept from neighboring pagans. Angelology has other such examples. The Babylonian name for an angel is, for instance, "watcher." Aside from one or two nonangelic uses, the only place the term appears in Scripture is in Daniel, twice on the lips of Babylonian king Nebuchadnezzar (4.13, 17) and once from Daniel referring to what the king had told him (4.23). But ancient Jews adopted the designation, as did later Christians. The *Legend of the Watchers*, found in the pseudepigraphal book of *Enoch*, makes use of the term, for instance, as do the poems of Ephraim the Syrian.

 So did the ancients merely smuggle pagan notions into Judaism and Christianity, or is something else happening here?

I think we can answer that question by posing another one: If the God of Jews and Christians is real and his story reliable, shouldn't we expect to see this sort of overlap? Assuming angels are real, it is also reasonable to assume that an experience of the will be universal, not merely restricted to those who believe Moses and Jesus. Moses and Jesus make claims about the world that transcend those who believe them and bear upon even those who disbelieve. So to find overlap shows not borrowing but rather a predictable, common experience among many peoples.

God gave his angels "jurisdiction" over the peoples of the earth, something we'll explore later in chapter 3 and again at the start of chapter 4. The fact that Jews held captive in Babylon began using the Babylonian name for angels only suggests that they recognized the reality and influence of the angels operating in Babylon. Cross-cultural interaction enhanced and expanded their view, but it did not invent it.

46. Ezekiel 1.15–21; 10.9–14; Daniel 7.9.
47. Deuteronomy 32.8. *The New English Translation of the Septuagint* (NETS) uses "divine sons" here, while Charles Lee Brenton's classic translation more clearly employs "angels of God," an understanding that seems readily ratified by the ancient commentators. Regarding angelic princes, Daniel 10.13, 20–21; 12.1.
48. Clement of Alexandria, *Miscellanies* 6.17.
49. John Damascene, *Exposition* 2.3.
50. *The Annunciation*, in Bussagli, *Angels*, 560.
51. *Jacob's Ladder*, in Bussagli, *Angels*, 172.
52. Pseudo-Dionysius, *Celestial Hierarchy* 4.2.
53. Isaac the Syrian, *Ascetical Homilies* 28.
54. Regarding angelic control in nature, John 5.4 introduces us to the angel who stirs the pool of Bethesda, and

Revelation 16.5 similarly indicates an "angel of water."
Revelation 14.18 features an angel with power over fire,
while 7.1 shows a group of angels controlling the winds.
An illuminated copy of Beatus of Liébana's eighth-century
Commentary on the Apocalypse illustrates this verse with four
angels stationed in the four corners of the page, each with
winds gusting from their mouths. See page 20 of the
present work.

55. Athenagoras, *Plea* 24.

56. Hermas, *Shepherd of Hermas*, Commandments 6.2.

57. Basil, *On the Holy Spirit* 38.

58. Genesis 18.4; 19.2; 32.24–26.

59. Augustine, *Handbook* 59.

60. Daniel 8.17; 10.5–6.

61. Ephraim the Syrian said that Daniel's nature melted
    before the angel like wax melts before fire. Gabriel was
    not dreadful or wrathful, but his nature—full of "awful
    majesty"—was simply too much for Daniel to bear. *On Our
    Lord* 27.

62. Isaiah 6.1–5.

63. Daniel 10.11.

64. Genesis 16.6–13.

65. Hebrews 13.2.

66. Augustine, *Expositions on the Psalms* 86.11.

67. Ignatius, *Trallians* 5. While his point precludes sharing
    details, Ignatius has a vision of heaven and angels. Church
    historian Socrates of Constantinople later refers to the
    experience in *Ecclesiastical History* 6.8.

68. In 2 Corinthians 12.2–4 Paul says, "I know a man in
    Christ who fourteen years ago was caught up to the third
    heaven—whether in the body or out of the body I do not
    know, God knows. And I know that this man was caught

up into Paradise—whether in the body or out of the
body I do not know, God knows—and he heard things
that cannot be told, which man may not utter." Church
tradition holds that these verses are autobiographical but
that Paul was too modest to mention himself. The ancient
commentators consistently assign the experience to the
apostle himself. See, for instance, Methodius, *Discourse on
the Resurrection* 3.9, and Augustine, *Homilies on the Gospel of John*
7.23.

Chapter 2. Falls from Grace

1. That the Christian concept of evil (as personalized in
   the character of Satan and all those who supposedly side
   with him) is fundamentally an empty projection and
   rationalization is the main (and unconvincing) point of
   Elaine Pagels's book *The Origin of Satan* (New York: Vintage,
   1996).
2. Irenaeus, *Against Heresies* 4.40.
3. Job 4.18; 15.15; 2 Peter 2.4; Jude 1.6.
4. Gregory of Nazianzen, *Orations* 38.9.
5. John Damascene, *Exposition* 2.4.
6. Origen, *On First Principles*, preface.
7. Genesis 2.15–17; 3.
8. Revelation 12.9.
9. Justin Martyr, *Dialogue* 45, 79, 100, 103, 124–25.
10. Irenaeus, *On the Apostolic Preaching* 1.1.16. Additional
    examples of writers identifying Satan with the serpent
    include Irenaeus, *Against Heresies* 3.23.1–7, and Ephraim
    the Syrian, *Nisibene Hymns* 35.20; 57.4. One strength of
    Irenaeus's view, as articulated in *On the Apostolic Preaching*,
    is that if the serpent were an actual participant in the
    fraud, then his actions explain God's subsequent curse. If

the serpent were not somehow morally culpable by active cooperation with Satan, the curse would seem unjust.

11. *Life of Adam and Eve*, pericope 18, Slavonic.

12. Genesis 3.1, 14. Regarding the linguistic connection between serpents and seraphim: making this connection to the story of deception in Eden adds color and possibly context to the apostle Paul's warning about Satan's coming as an angel of light.

13. Wisdom 2.23–24.

14. Irenaeus, *On the Apostolic Preaching* 1.1.16.

15. Cyprian, *Treatises* 10.

16. *Life of Adam and Eve*, pericopes 5 and 18.

17. Augustine, *Homilies on the Gospel of John* 17.16.

18. 1 Timothy 3.6.

19. That pride is the source of sin comes from Sirach 10.13, though some translations reverse the point and say that sin is the source of pride. As far as moral reasoning, I suppose we are in chicken-and-egg territory. For Augustine's thinking on pride and its relation to envy, see *The Literal Meaning of Genesis* 11.14–16. Drawing a distinction or sequence between pride and envy is tricky because one is personal and the other is social, but as persons we are incapable of living outside society—and it's the same with the angels. God is everywhere present and fills all things, so Satan's pride would by necessity express itself in envy the same moment it arose because he could not escape the presence, the society, of God.

20. Gregory of Nyssa, *The Great Catechism* 6.

21. Ibid.

22. Ibid.

23. Augustine, *Homilies on the Gospel of John* 17.16.

24. John Cassian, *Conferences* 8.8–10.

25. Ezekiel 28.1–19 NKJV. There is an alternate reading for Ezekiel 28 that many translations, including the *Revised Standard Version* (RSV) and NETS, favor. In this reading, the subject isn't the cherub but is rather someone placed in the care of a cherub (v. 14), who later drives the figure from the mountain of God (v. 16), an image that fits well with the already established role of cherubim guarding Eden.

26. Isaiah 14.3–23.

27. Tertullian, *Against Marcion* 5.11; Origen, *Homilies on Ezekiel* 1.3.7–8, 13. It's also worth noting how Augustine absorbs and applies this interpretation in *The Literal Meaning of Genesis* 11.24–25.

28. Prudentius, *The Origin of Sin*.

29. *Life of Adam and Eve*, pericope 5. See also Gary A. Anderson, "Ezekiel 28, the Fall of Satan, and the Adam Books," in *Literature on Adam and Eve*, ed. Gary A. Anderson et al. (London: Brill, 2000).

30. Another wrinkle: many ancient Jews and Christians believed that the angels fell because of lust. "[T]he sons of God saw that the daughters of men were fair," as it says in Genesis 6.2, "and they took to wife such of them as they chose." This view separates the fall of Satan and that of the other angels. Satan's envy and pride first got the better of him, while the angels later succumbed to lust, only following Satan after God punished them for their sin. These angels, said Athenagoras of Athens, "fell into impure love of virgins, and . . . became negligent and wicked in the management of the things entrusted to [them]." *Plea* 24.

    It may sound outlandish to readers today, but many authorities in the early church held this view, including Irenaeus, Justin Martyr, Tertullian, Clement of Alexandria,

Archelaus of Mesopotamia, and many others. It's possible that Jude's epistle provided warrant to advocates of the view, since Jude quotes from the extrabiblical book of *Enoch*, a work that drew from Genesis 6 and elaborated a tale of angelic libido and heavenly rebellion. It's even possible that Jude held this view, but since neither Jude nor the portion of *Enoch* he quotes deals directly with this material, it's not certain. Nor for that matter is it considered an official Christian teaching, despite some of its prominent proponents. Origen, for instance, observed that the *Enoch* literature was not universally circulated among Christian congregations, and wide circulation was the norm for books considered canonical by the young church; the gap indicates a lack of universal acceptance. *Against Celsus* 5.54.

Though, that said, the Alexandrine text of the Septuagint renders Genesis 6.2 as explicitly as "angels of God," not "sons," indicating such a belief by those following that textual tradition—and Genesis was certainly read and expounded in church.

Later authorities distanced themselves from this interpretation, adopting instead a more naturalistic reading, understanding "sons of God" to mean the righteous lineage of Seth, while "daughters of men" pointed to the lineage of the manslayer Cain. John Cassian adopted and promulgated this understanding, as did Augustine and most who came after. Since neither interpretation runs counter to the rule of faith, such differences should not distress so much as entertain and inform.

31. 2 Peter 2.4 NKJV.

32. Luke 10.18.

33. Revelation 12.4, 9.

34. Ephesians 2.2—and notice the connection later in

the letter to the battle "against the spiritual hosts of wickedness in the heavenly places" (6.12). For the composition of the world according to the ancients, see C. S. Lewis, *The Discarded Image* (London: Cambridge University Press, 1964).

35. John Chrysostom, *Homilies on Ephesians* 4.
36. Prudentius, *The Origin of Sin*.
37. John Cassian, *Conferences* 8.12.
38. Ibid.
39. Daniel 10.13, 20; Ephesians 6.12.
40. John Cassian, *Conferences* 8.12.
41. *Epistle of Barnabas* 4, 20.
42. Augustine, *Homilies on the Gospel of John* 110.7.
43. John Damascene, *Exposition* 2.3.
44. Augustine, *Homilies on the Gospel of John* 110.7.
45. Mark the Monk, *On the Incarnation* 32.
46. Prudentius, *The Origin of Sin*.

Chapter 3. Celestial Stewards

1. Basil, *On the Origin of Humanity*, Discourse 1.8.
2. John Chrysostom, *Homilies on Ephesians* 4.
3. See, for instance, John 12.31; 14.30; 16.11; Ephesians 2.2; 2 Corinthians 4.4.
4. Ephraim the Syrian, *Hymns on the Nativity* 14.11.
5. Cyril of Alexandria, *A Commentary Upon the Gospel According to S. Luke* 64. See also Eusebius of Caesarea, *Proof of the Gospel* 4.9, and Gregory Nazianzen, *Orations* 28.15.
6. Irenaeus, *Against Heresies* 5.24.
7. Pseudo-Dionysius, *Celestial Hierarchy* 9.4.
8. Genesis 12.1–4.
9. Genesis 18.1–15.
10. Genesis 18.16–19.29.

11. See Deuteronomy 28; Romans 6.23.

12. Genesis 22.1–18.

13. Genesis 24.40.

14. Genesis 27.1–28.17.

15. Ephraim the Syrian, *Commentary on Genesis* 26.1–2.

16. Genesis 31.11–13.

17. Genesis 32.1–2.

18. Ephraim the Syrian, *Commentary on Genesis* 30.1.

19. Genesis 32.24–32; Hosea 12.4.

20. Ephraim the Syrian, *Commentary on Genesis* 30.3.

21. Genesis 48.16.

22. Exodus 3.2–5; 14.19–25; Isaiah 63.9.

23. Augustine, *On the Trinity* 3.11. Exodus 19.3–6; Acts 7.38, 53; Galatians 3.19. See also Pseudo-Dionysius, *Celestial Hierarchy* 4.2–3.

24. Pseudo-Dionysius, *Celestial Hierarchy* 4.3.

25. Judges 6.12–14.

26. Despite the usual understanding of the second commandment, Jews did in fact utilize imagery in their places of worship, Dura-Europos being one significant example. But their representations differed from Christian ones. One major difference between Christian and Jewish icons of Moses and the burning bush involves the extended hand of God. In the Jewish icon, God's fingers are merely outstretched; in the Christian icon, the fingers form the sign of the cross, showing the Christian conviction that Christ is God.

27. Exodus 23.20–22; Daniel 10.21.

28. Numbers 22–24. Susan R. Garrett makes this same observation about the blind seer in her book *No Ordinary Angel* (New Haven: Yale University Press, 2008), 20.

29. Exodus 16; Numbers 11.7–9; Psalm 78.25; Wisdom

16.20–21. See also Revelation 2.14–17, which alludes to the mystical quality of the manna, something covered in depth in chapter 6.

30. Joshua 5.13–15; Exodus 23.23–33.

31. Judges 2.1–5.

32. See, for instance, 1 Corinthians 10.20; Deuteronomy 32.17; Leviticus 17.7; Psalm 106.37. Psalm 95.5 (96.5) in the Septuagint says, "[T]he gods of the nations are demons" (NETS).

33. Prudentius, *On the Origin of Sin*.

34. Judges 13.3–21; 6.12–14; Isaiah 6.6–8.

35. 1 Kings 19.1–8.

36. Mark 3.22; Matthew 12.24–27; Luke 11.15–19.

37. 2 Kings 1.2–4.

38. 2 Kings 1.15–17.

39. Psalm 34.7.

40. Psalm 90.5–6, 10–12 (91.5–6, 10–12) NETS.

41. 2 Kings 6.11–17.

42. Revelation 12.10.

43. Job 1–2.

44. Zechariah 3.1–5.

45. Job 33.23–26. This is a difficult passage, and various translations render it differently, sometimes significantly so. The presentation here seems, however, in keeping with the rest of the witness on angelic advocates, particularly if we understand their ultimate function is to illuminate Christ as our advocate.

46. John Chrysostom, *Homilies on the Statutes* 1.18.

47. Ambrose, *Letters* 34.10.

48. 2 Kings 19.35; 2 Chronicles 32.21; Isaiah 37.36.

49. Exodus 4.24–26 NETS. The Septuagint and the Masoretic differ here. The latter says that God came to kill him,

while the Septuagint identifies the angel of God. Both are true, but the Septuagint has the virtue of saying more clearly *how* God came—that is, through the presence of an angel, as he does so often in the Scripture.

50. Origen, *On First Principles* 3.2.1.

51. Augustine, *Letters* 23.

52. Maximus the Confessor, *Ad Thalassium* 17.

53. Ephraim the Syrian, *Commentary on Exodus* 4.3–4. See also Gregory of Nyssa, *The Life of Moses* 1.22; 2.3.

54. Exodus 30.

55. 1 Chronicles 21.1–16. See also 2 Samuel 24.1–17.

56. Ambrose, *Letters* 34.

57. See Deuteronomy 28.36, 41, 64.

58. Daniel 3.

59. Daniel 6; 14.31–39. This second passage is part of the Bel and the Dragon story and may go under different numbering in some Bibles—or, regrettably, be left out entirely. See also Prudentius, *Daily Round* 4. If the reader is struck by the apparent outlandishness of the Habakkuk story, remember that Ezekiel was similarly upborne, and Philip was whisked away by the Spirit after baptizing the Ethiopian eunuch. Ezekiel 8.3; Acts 8.39.

60. Ezekiel 1.24.

61. Ezekiel 3.17–21.

62. Ezekiel 8.

63. Ezekiel 9–10.

64. Daniel 2.26–49. Note the comparison to Joseph: Genesis 41.

65. Daniel 4:13–17.

66. Daniel 4.19–37.

67. Daniel 7.1–14.

68. Daniel 7.15–28.

69. Daniel 8.15–27.
70. Daniel 9.21–23.
71. Daniel 10.
72. Zechariah 12.8.
73. Zechariah 13.1; 12.10.
74. *Epistle to Diognetus* 7.2.

CHAPTER 4. LORD OF THE ANGELS

1. John 1.51.
2. Augustine, *Homilies on the Gospel of John* 7.23; 121.1.
3. Psalm 78.25; Wisdom 16.20–21.
4. *The Protoevangelium of James* 7–9.
5. *The Annunciation* in Alfredo Tradigo, *Icons and Saints of the Eastern Orthodox Church*, trans. Stephen Sartarelli (Los Angeles: J. Paul Getty Museum, 2006), 101–3; John Beckwith, *Early Christian and Byzantine Art*, 2nd ed. (New York: Penguin, 1979), 243, 252, 273; Irmgard Hutter, *Early Christian and Byzantine*, trans. Alistair Laing (New York: Universe, 1988), 171.
6. Luke 1.42.
7. Luke 1.30–33.
8. Luke 1.38.
9. Luke 1.11–19.
10. Matthew 1.18–25.
11. Luke 1.19.
12. Tobit 12.15.
13. Revelation 1.4; 5.6; 8.2.
14. Papias, Fragment 9.
15. Eusebius, *Proof of the Gospel* 4.10.
16. Ephraim the Syrian, *Hymns on the Nativity* 5.
17. Luke 2.14 NKJV.
18. Ephraim the Syrian, *Hymns on the Nativity* 1.

19. Origen, *Commentary on the Gospel of John* I.13.

20. Revelation 12.1–4.

21. Matthew 2.16.

22. Matthew 2.13.

23. Matthew 2.19–21.

24. Cyril of Alexandria, *A Commentary Upon the Gospel According to S. Luke* 3.

25. It also hearkens back to Moses' forty-day fast on Mount Sinai while receiving the law of God, Exodus 34.28, showing that Christ was both a new lawgiver and a new liberator.

26. Matthew 4.3–10.

27. Luke 4.13.

28. Matthew 4.11.

29. Augustine, *Expositions on the Psalms* 57.8.

30. *The Baptism of Christ* in Hutter, *Early Christian and Byzantine*, 128; Beckwith, *Early Christian and Byzantine Art*, 61, 290; Tradigo, *Icons and Saints*, 122–23.

31. Mark 1.21–28 NKJV.

32. Matthew 8.28–33; Mark 5.1–21; Luke 8.26–39.

33. Matthew 9.32–33; 12.22.

34. Mark 9.14–29; Luke 4.38–41; 13.11–16.

35. Matthew 9.32–34; 12.22–28; see also Matthew 12.26, 28; Mark 3.22–26; Luke 11.14–19.

36. Mark 1.24 NKJV.

37. Ephraim the Syrian, *Hymns on the Nativity* 3.

38. Matthew 10.1, 7–8; see also Mark 3.15–16; 6.7; Luke 10.1–16.

39. Cyril of Alexandria, *A Commentary Upon the Gospel According to S. Luke* 60. The root of this idea goes back to the notion of seventy nations throughout the world from the seventy descendants of Noah, per Genesis 10, as well as allusions to the twelve tribes of Israel (springs of water) and seventy

nations (palm trees) in Exodus 15.27 and Numbers 33.9. Folding one passage over another here produces a layered picture that concerns not only people but also angels. From Deuteronomy and Daniel we know that God set angelic princes over the nations. Working from Genesis 10, we number those angelic princes at seventy. In Psalm 82 and Job 1–2 we see God sitting amid these angelic overseers in council. But the angels failed in their administration of the nations. Satan usurped their territories, as Eusebius says in *Proof of the Gospel* 4.9. Christ came, as we saw, to redeem the nations and complete the job the angels were unable to manage, and his seventy disciples lead us to contemplate Christ's mission spreading to all the peoples whose oversight the demons had usurped.

40. Luke 10.20.
41. Cyril of Alexandria, *A Commentary Upon the Gospel According to S. Luke* 65.
42. Note Paul's similar concern in 1 Timothy 3.6.
43. Luke 10.18.
44. Cyril of Alexandria, *A Commentary Upon the Gospel According to S. Luke* 65.
45. Revelation 12.7–9 NKJV.
46. John 12.31.
47. Luke 22.31.
48. John 13.27. This was not possession against Judas's will. Like the serpent in the Garden, Judas was a willing collaborator.
49. John 12.5–6.
50. *The Services of Great and Holy Week and Pascha*, Kathisma (Tone 3) for Bridegroom Orthros of Holy Wednesday.
51. Luke 22.43.
52. Ephraim the Syrian, *On Our Lord* 38.

53. *The Crucifixion* in Tradigo, *Icons and Saints*, 137–38; Beckwith, *Early Christian and Byzantine Art*, 285.

54. Prudentius, *Daily Round* 9. In the messianic or christological understanding of the early church, the Psalter speaks to the same event: "Raise the gates, O rulers of yours! And be raised up, O perpetual gates! And the King of glory shall enter" (Psalm 23.7 NETS). The Eastern Orthodox Church retains this connection in its paschal matins service, which ties the passage to Christ's victory over death and the grave.

55. Mark 3.27; Matthew 12.29.

56. *The Harrowing of Hell*, in Hutter, *Early Christian and Byzantine*, 145, 173–74; Beckwith, *Early Christian and Byzantine Art*, 231, 235, 255, 318; Tradigo, *Icons and Saints*, 143–44. In the matins service mentioned in note 54, a version of this icon greets worshippers as they reenter the church following the priest's recitation of the psalm outside the door of the church.

57. Ephraim the Syrian, *Nisibene Hymns* 60.31.

58. Matthew 28.2–4.

59. Acts 1.6–11.

60. John 3.5.

61. See Gregory of Nyssa, *The Life of Moses* 2.120–21, 124–26.

62. John the Deacon, *Letter to Senarius* 3.

63. Tertullian, *The Shows* 4.

64. Tertullian, *The Crown* 3.

65. Hippolytus, *On the Apostolic Tradition* 20.

66. Ibid. 21.

67. Cyril of Jerusalem, *Catechetical Lectures* 3.3.

68. 1 Peter 1.12.

69. Luke 15.10.

70. Gregory Nazianzen, *Orations* 38.14.

71. Cyril of Jerusalem, *Catechetical Lectures* 3.16.

72. Ephraim the Syrian, *Epiphany Hymns* 6.
73. Cyril of Jerusalem, *Catechetical Lectures*, procatechesis 15.
74. Zechariah 3.1–4.
75. Revelation 12.10.
76. Ephraim the Syrian, *Epiphany Hymns* 13.
77. Ibid.
78. Ibid.
79. Ibid.

CHAPTER 5. GUARDIANS OF SOUL AND BODY

1. *The Life of Macarius of Scetis* 8.
2. *The Virtues of Saint Macarius* 1.
3. Ambrose, *Sermon Against Auxentius* 11.
4. *Byzantine Rite, Barberini Euchologion* fol. 170ff., a prayer after making one a catechumen.
5. See, for instance, *The Divine Liturgy of James*, Liturgy of the Catechumen.
6. Hebrews 1.14.
7. Acts 10.1–11.18.
8. Gregory of Nyssa, *The Life of Moses* 2.44.
9. Genesis 48.16.
10. Psalm 91.11–12.
11. Tobit 4–12.
12. Matthew 18.10.
13. Acts 8.26–38. In the classical world to which the evangelist Luke was writing, Ethiopia indicated not the present-day country but the Nubian kingdom of Kush and its capital city, Meroe, which sits just north of modern Ethiopia in Sudan.
14. Acts 5.19–20.
15. Revelation 12.17.
16. Acts 12.1–11. Sometime following this episode, God's long-suffering with Herod came to an end. Acts 12.23

reports, simply enough, "[A]n angel of the Lord smote him, because he did not give God the glory."

17. Acts 12.12–16.

18. Note Acts 12.15.

19. Acts 27.24.

20. John Chrysostom, *Homilies on the Acts of the Apostles* 26.

21. Ibid.

22. Basil, *On the Holy Spirit* 30.

23. Hermas, *Shepherd of Hermas*, Commandments 6.2.

24. Clement of Alexandria, *Miscellanies* 6.17.

25. Gregory Thaumaturgus, *Oration* 4.

26. *The Life of Macarius of Scetis* 15, 16, 18, 22, 27.

27. Isaac the Syrian, *Ascetical Homilies* 24.

28. Ibid. 5.

29. Gregory Thaumaturgus, *Oration* 4.

30. Origen, *On First Principles* 1.8.1. Revelation 2.1, 8.

31. Macarius of Alexandria, *First Syriac Epistle* 5.

32. *Epistle of Barnabas* 18.

33. Hermas, *Shepherd of Hermas*, Commandments 6.2.

34. John Cassian, *Conferences* 8.17.

35. Psalm 108.6 (109.6) HTM. The English word *devil* is the Hebrew *satan*. The King James renders the verse, "[L]et Satan stand at his right hand." Most modern translations opt for *accuser*, which is a serviceable choice since the psalm could here refer merely to a human accuser but doesn't preclude assuming something more—as did the early Christians. Peter linked this psalm to Judas (Acts 1.20), a prophetic invitation to see the accuser as the same one who possessed the backstabbing disciple (John 13.27), the same accuser who came against Job and the high priest Joshua, and who was thrown down by Michael (Revelation 12.7–10).

36. Gregory of Nyssa, *The Life of Moses* 2.46.
37. *Epistle of Barnabas* 21.
38. John Climacus, *The Ladder of Divine Ascent* 26.5.
39. Macarius of Alexandria, *First Syriac Epistle* 9.
40. See John Climacus, *The Ladder of Divine Ascent* 26.20.
41. Isaac the Syrian, *Ascetical Homilies* 39.
42. John Climacus, *The Ladder of Divine Ascent*, 15.69; see also 26.103.
43. Isaac the Syrian, *Ascetical Homilies* 39.
44. Gregory of Nyssa, *The Life of Moses* 2.47.
45. 1 Corinthians 10.13.
46. *The Life of Evagrius* 5–7. See also Palladius, *The Lausiac History* 38.3–7.
47. See *The Life of Macarius of Scetis* 22, 27.
48. See 2 Corinthians 12.7.
49. John Chrysostom, *Homilies on the Gospel of Matthew* 13.5.
50. Antiochus Strategos, "The Capture of Jerusalem by the Persians."
51. Isaac the Syrian, *Ascetical Homilies* 57.
52. John Chrysostom, *Homilies on Ephesians* 1.
53. Clement of Rome, *First Epistle* 34.
54. Bede, *Homilies on the Gospels* 2.10.

Chapter 6. Voices Ascending

1. Psalm 137.1 NETS.
2. See, for instance, Exodus 25.18–22; 26.1, 31; 36.8, 35; 37.7–9; Numbers 7.89.
3. *The Cherubim of the Ark of the Covenant*, in Marco Bussagli, *Angels*, trans. Rosanna M. Giammanco Frongia (New York: Abrams, 2007), 204.
4. Hebrews 8.5.
5. Galatians 3.24 NKJV.

6. Hebrews 12.22.

7. Revelation 1.1, 10.

8. Revelation 4.1–2, 5.

9. Revelation 1.12–13.

10. Tobit 12.15.

11. Luke 1.19.

12. Revelation 5.11.

13. Revelation 4.8; 5–6.

14. According to church historian Socrates of Constantinople, angels influenced the style of hymn singing of Christians in Antioch and then beyond to the whole church. Ignatius, the third bishop of the city, saw a vision of heaven in which "angels [were] hymning in alternate chants the Holy Trinity." Following the epiphany, Ignatius instructed the Antiochian church in antiphonal chanting, and the practice soon spread to other churches. *Ecclesiastical History* 6.8.

15. *The Divine Liturgy of James*, Liturgy of the Catechumen.

16. *The Divine Liturgy of James*, Anaphora.

17. *The Liturgy of the Blessed Apostles*, Anaphora.

18. Bede, *Homilies on the Gospels* 2.10.

19. "Cherubic Hymns," *The Great Horologion*.

20. *The Divine Liturgy of James*, Liturgy of the Faithful.

21. "Cherubic Hymns," *The Great Horologion*.

22. Cyril of Jerusalem, *Catechetical Lectures* 23.6.

23. John Chrysostom, *Homilies on the Epistle to the Hebrews* 16.6.

24. John Chrysostom, *On the Priesthood* 6.4.

25. Symeon d-Taibutha, *The Book of Grace* 1.84.

26. *The Divine Liturgy of the Holy Apostle and Evangelist Mark*, Prayer of Oblation.

27. John Chrysostom, *On the Priesthood* 6.4.

28. *The Life of Macarius of Alexandria* 20.

29. Ibid. 16. See also Palladius, *The Lausiac History* 18.25; Sozomen, *Ecclesiastical History* 6.29.

30. J. W. Appell, *Monuments of Early Christian Art* (London: Eyre and Spottiswoode, 1872), 31–32.

31. Bel and the Dragon (Old Greek) 33 NETS. Compare with Daniel 14.31–39. For an example in art: *The Angel Leads Habbacuc to Daniel in the Lions' Den*, in Bussagli, *Angels*, 442–43.

32. Psalm 78.24–25.

33. Wisdom 16.20– 21.

34. Augustine, *Expositions on the Psalms* 78.15.

35. Ibid. 135.4

36. John Damascene, *Exposition* 2.3.

37. Augustine, *Expositions on the Psalms* 135.4.

38. Matthew 4.4.

39. John 6.51, 53–54.

40. Augustine, *Expositions on the Psalms* 135.4.

41. Augustine, *Sermons on Selected Lessons of the New Testament* 7.7.

42. Augustine, *Expositions on the Psalms* 135.4.

43. Symeon d-Taibutha, *The Book of Grace* 1.84.

44. John Climacus, *The Ladder of Divine Ascent* 28.1.

45. Tobit 12.12, 15.

46. Aphrahat, *Demonstrations* 4.

47. Revelation 8.3–4.

48. Isaac the Syrian, *Ascetical Homilies* 24.

49. Clement of Alexandria, *Miscellanies* 7.7.

50. Quoted in Anonymous I, "On Prayer."

51. Ambrose, *Concerning Widows* 9.

52. Most famously, Paul in Colossians 2.18.

53. Augustine, *Sermons on Selected Lessons of the New Testament* 33.4.

54. John Chrysostom, *Homilies on the Epistle to the Hebrews* 27.8.

55. Evagrius, *Admonition on Prayer*.

56. John Climacus, *The Ladder of Divine Ascent* 21.12.

57. Ibid. 28.11.

58. Isaac the Syrian, *Ascetical Homilies* 3.

59. Aphrahat, *Demonstrations* 13.

60. Compare with Matthew 5.23–24 about bringing offerings while being at odds with one's brother.

61. John Climacus, *The Ladder of Divine Ascent* 28.7.

62. Palladius, *The Lausiac History* 32.1, 6–7.

63. John Damascene, *Exposition* 3.10.

64. John Climacus, *The Ladder of Divine Ascent* 5.29–31.

65. Martyrius, *Book of Perfection* 70.

66. John Climacus, *The Ladder of Divine Ascent* 20.19; 28.63.

67. Ibid. 27.9.

Chapter 7. Final Companions

1. According to Origen, the story of Moses' body is also found in the Jewish pseudepigraphal book *The Ascension* [or *Assumption*] *of Moses. On First Principles* 3.2.1.

2. 2 Corinthians 5.8 NKJV.

3. Luke 16.22.

4. Asterius of Amasea, "The Rich Man and Lazarus."

5. Bede, *Ecclesiastical History* 3.8.

6. Bede, *Ecclesiastical History* 3.19. Fursey was burned on the return passage in the vision, something that affected him thereafter and enabled deeper, more thorough repentance for his sins.

7. John Chrysostom, *Homilies on the Gospel of Matthew* 4.19.

8. Psalm 116.15.

9. John Chrysostom, *On the Priesthood* 6.4.

10. See, for instance, *Death of Saint Procopius of Ustiug*, in Alfredo Tradigo, *Icons and Saints of the Eastern Orthodox Church*, trans. Stephen Sartarelli (Los Angeles: J. Paul Getty Museum, 2006), 353.

11. "How Souls Travel to Heaven," in Part 2 of *Stories, Sermons, and Prayers of St. Nephon: An Ascetic Bishop*.

12. Ambrose, *Letters* 15.

13. Matthew 24.31, 36.

14. Matthew 13.37–43, 49–50; 25.41.

15. 1 Thessalonians 4.16; 2 Thessalonians 1.7–8.

16. 1 Timothy 5.21; 1 Corinthians 4.9; Basil, *On the Holy Spirit* 29.

17. Matthew 16.27.

18. *The Lord Separates the Sheep from the Goats*, in Marco Bussagli, *Angels*, trans. Rosanna M. Giammanco Frongia (New York: Abrams, 2007), 516.

19. Ignatius, *Smyrneans* 6.

20. 1 Corinthians 6.3.

21. Theodoret of Cyrus, *The First Letter to the Corinthians* 6.

22. Augustine, *City of God* 14.11.

23. C. S. Lewis, *A Preface to Paradise Lost* (London: Oxford University Press, 1943), 66.

24. John Chrysostom, *Three Homilies Concerning the Power of Demons* 1.8.

25. "More heaven than hell" comes from a lyric penned by Jerry Gaskill, Doug Pinnick, Ty Tabor, and Sam Taylor.

26. Augustine, *Expositions on the Psalms* 86.23. While often abused in popular culture, the notion of playing harps in heaven goes back to the book of Revelation. Take, for instance, the second verse of chapter 15: "[T]hose that conquered the beast . . . [stood] beside the sea of glass with harps of God in their hands." See also Revelation 5.8; 14.2; and 18.22.

Bibliography

All sources arranged by first name or first key term. Note the following abbreviations.

ACW	*Ancient Christian Writers,* Paulist Press
ANF	*Ante-Nicene Fathers*
CS	*Cistercian Studies,* Cistercian Publications
CWS	*Classics of Western Spirituality,* Paulist Press
FOC	*Fathers of the Church,* Catholic University of America Press
LCL	*Loeb Classical Library,* Harvard University Press
LOF	*A Library of Fathers of the Holy Catholic Church*
NPNF	*Nicene and Post-Nicene Fathers*
PPS	*Popular Patristics Series,* St. Vladimir's Seminary Press
SBLEJL	*Society of Biblical Literature, Early Judaism and Its Literature*

Ambrose, *Concerning Widows,* trans. H. De Romestin, *NPNF* 2.10.
———, *The Letters of S. Ambrose,* trans. H. Walford, *LOF.*

————, *Sermon Against Auxentius*, in *The Letters of S. Ambrose*, trans. H. Walford, *LOF*.

Anonymous I, "On Prayer," trans. Sebastian Brock, *CS* 101.

Antiochus Strategos, "The Capture of Jerusalem by the Persians," trans. Frederick C. Conybeare, *English Historical Review* 25 (1910).

Aphrahat, *Demonstrations*, trans. John Gwynn, *NPNF* 2.13.

Asterius of Amasea, "The Rich Man and Lazarus," in Galusha Anderson and Edgar Johnson Goodspeed, trans., *Ancient Sermons for Modern Times* (New York: Pilgrim Press, 1904).

Athenagoras, *A Plea for the Christians*, trans. B. P. Pratten, *ANF* 2.

Augustine, *City of God*, trans. Henry Bettenson (New York: Penguin, 1984).

————, *Expositions on the Psalms*, ed. A. Cleveland Coxe, *NPNF* 1.8.

————, *Handbook* [or *Enchiridion*], trans. J. F. Shaw, *NPNF* 1.3.

————, *Homilies on the Gospel of John*, trans. John Gibb and James Innes, *NPNF* 1.7.

————, *The Letters of St. Augustine*, trans. J. G. Cunningham, *NPNF* 1.1.

————, *The Literal Meaning of Genesis*, trans. John Hammond Taylor, *ACW* 41–42.

————, *On Christian Doctrine*, trans. J. F. Shaw, *NPNF* 1.2.

————, *On the Trinity*, trans. Arthur West Haddan, *NPNF* 1.3.

————, *Sermons on Selected Lessons of the New Testament*, trans. R. G. MacMullen, *NPNF* 1.6.

Basil, *The Hexaemeron*, trans. Blomfield Jackson, *NPNF* 2.8.

————, *On the Holy Spirit*, trans. Stephen Hildebrand, *PPS* 42.

————, *On the Origin of Humanity*, trans. Nonna Verna Harrison, *PPS* 30.

Bede, *Ecclesiastical History of the English People*, trans. Leo Sherley-Price (New York: Penguin, 1990).

————, *Homilies on the Gospels*, trans. Lawrence T. Martin and David Hurst, *CS* 110–11.

The Book of Jubilees, in R. H. Charles, trans., *The Apocrypha and Pseudepigrapha of the Old Testament*, vol. 2 (London: Oxford University Press, 1913).

Byzantine Rite, in E. C. Whitaker and Maxwell E. Johnson, trans., *Documents of the Baptismal Liturgy*, 3rd ed. (Collegeville: Liturgical Press, 2003).

"Cherubic Hymns," *The Great Horologion* (Boston: Holy Transfiguration Monastery, 1997).

Clement of Alexandria, *Miscellanies* [or *Stromata*], trans. Alexander Roberts and James Donaldson, *ANF* 2.

Clement of Rome, *First Epistle*, trans. Bart D. Ehrman, *LCL* 24.

Cyprian, *The Treatises of Cyprian*, trans. Ernest Wallis, *ANF* 5.

Cyril of Alexandria, *A Commentary Upon the Gospel According to S. Luke*, vols. 1 and 2, trans. R. Payne Smith (Oxford: Oxford University Press, 1859).

Cyril of Jerusalem, *The Catechetical Lectures*, trans. Edward Hamilton Gifford, *NPNF* 2.7.

The Divine Liturgy of the Holy Apostle and Evangelist Mark, trans. George Ross Merry, *ANF* 7.

The Divine Liturgy of James, trans. William MacDonald, *ANF* 7.

Ephraim the Syrian, *Commentary on Genesis*, trans. Edward G. Matthews and Joseph P. Amar, *FOC* 91.

————, *Commentary on Exodus*, trans. Edward G. Matthews and Joseph P. Amar, *FOC* 91.

————, *Epiphany Hymns*, trans. Albert Edward Johnston, *NPNF* 2.13.

————, *Hymns on the Nativity*, trans. J. B. Morris and Albert Edward Johnston, *NPNF* 2.13.

————, *Nisibene Hymns*, trans. Joseph T. Sarsfield, *NPNF* 2.13.

————, *On Our Lord*, trans. A. Edward Johnston, *NPNF* 2.13.

Eusebius, *The Proof of the Gospel*, trans. W. J. Ferrar (Eugene: Wipf and Stock, 2001).

Epistle of Barnabas, trans. Bart D. Ehrman, *LCL* 25.

Epistle to Diognetus, trans. Bart D. Ehrman, *LCL* 25.

Evagrius, *Admonition on Prayer*, trans. Sebastian Brock, *CS* 101.

Gregory Nazianzen, "Concerning Spiritual Beings," trans. Peter Gilbert, *PPS* 21.

————, *Orations*, trans. Charles Gordon Browne and James Edward Swallow, *NPNF* 2.7.

Gregory Thaumaturgus, *Oration and Panegyric Addressed to Origen*, trans. S. D. F. Salmond, *ANF* 6.

Gregory of Nyssa, *The Great Catechism*, trans. William Moore and Henry Austin Wilson, *NPNF* 2.5.

————, *The Life of Moses*, trans. Abraham J. Malherbe and Everett Ferguson, *CWS*.

Hermas, *The Shepherd of Hermas*, trans. Bart D. Ehrman, *LCL* 25.

Hippolytus, *On the Apostolic Tradition*, trans. Alistair Stewart-Sykes, *PPS* 22.

Ignatius, *Smyrneans*, trans. Bart D. Ehrman, *LCL* 24.

————, *Trallians*, trans. Bart D. Ehrman, *LCL* 24.

Irenaeus, *Against Heresies*, trans. Alexander Roberts and William H. Rambaut, *ANF* 1.

————, *On the Apostolic Preaching*, trans. John Behr, *PPS* 17.

Isaac the Syrian, *The Ascetical Homilies*, trans. Dana R. Miller (Boston: Holy Transfiguration Monastery, 1984).

Jerome, *Apology*, trans. Earnest Cushing Richardson, *NPNF* 2.3.

John Cassian, *Conferences*, trans. Edgar C. S. Gibson, *NPNF* 2.11.

John Chrysostom, *Homilies on the Acts of the Apostles*, trans. J. Walker et al., *NPNF* 1.11.

————, *Homilies on Ephesians*, ed. Gross Alexander, *NPNF* 1.13.

————, *Homilies on the Epistle to the Hebrews*, ed. Frederic Gardiner, *NPNF* 1.14.

————, *Homilies on the Gospel of Matthew*, ed. M. B. Riddle, *NPNF* I.10.

————, *Homilies on the Statutes*, ed. W. R. W. Stephens, *NPNF* I.9.

————, *On the Priesthood*, trans. W. R. W. Stephens, *NPNF* I.9.

————, *Three Homilies Concerning the Power of Demons*, trans. T. P. Brandram, *NPNF* I.9.

John Climacus, *The Ladder of Divine Ascent*, trans. Lazarus Moore (Boston: Holy Transfiguration Monastery, 1991).

John Damascene, *Exposition of the Orthodox Faith*, trans. S. D. F. Salmond, *NPNF* 2.9.

John the Deacon, *Letter to Senarius*, in E. C. Whitaker and Maxwell E. Johnson, trans., *Documents of the Baptismal Liturgy*, 3rd ed. (Collegeville: Liturgical Press, 2003).

Justin Martyr, *Dialogue with Trypho*, trans. Marcus Dods and George Reith, *ANF* I.

The Life of Adam and Eve, ed. Gary A. Anderson and Michael E. Stone, *SBLEJL* 17.

The Life of Evagrius, trans. Tim Vivian, *PPS* 27.

The Life of Macarius of Alexandria, trans. Tim Vivian, *PPS* 27.

The Life of Macarius of Scetis, trans. Tim Vivian, *PPS* 28.

The Liturgy of the Blessed Apostles, trans. James Donaldson, *ANF* 7.

Macarius of Alexandria, *The First Syriac Epistle*, trans. Dana R. Miller, in Isaac the Syrian, *Ascetical Homilies* (Boston: Holy Transfiguration Monastery, 1984), Appendix C.

Mark the Monk, *On the Incarnation*, trans. Tim Vivian and Augustine Casiday, *PPS* 37.

Martyrius, *Book of Perfection*, trans. Sebastian Brock, *CS* 101.

Maximus the Confessor, *Ad Thalassium*, trans. Paul M. Blowers, *PPS* 25.

Methodius, *Discourse on the Resurrection*, trans. William R. Clark, *ANF* 6.

Origen, *Against Celsus*, trans. Allan Menzies, *ANF* 9.

———, *Commentary on the Gospel of John*, trans. Allan Menzies, *ANF* 9.

———, *Homilies on Ezekiel*, trans. Thomas P. Scheck, *ACW* 62.

———, *On First Principles* [or *De Principiis*], trans. Frederick Crombie, *ANF* 4.

Palladius, *The Lausiac History*, in W. K. Lowther Clarke, trans., *The Lausiac History of Palladius* (New York: Macmillan, 1918).

Papias, "Fragments," trans. Bart D. Ehrman, *LCL* 25.

The Protoevangelium of James, trans. Alexander Walker, *ANF* 8.

Prudentius, *The Daily Round*, trans. H. J. Thomson, *LCL* 387.

———, *The Origin of Sin*, trans. H. J. Thomson, *LCL* 387.

Pseudo-Dionysius, *The Celestial Hierarchy*, trans. Colm Luibheid, *CWS*.

The Services of Great and Holy Week and Pascha, ed. Joseph Rahal (Englewood: Antakya Press, 2006).

Socrates of Constantinople, *Ecclesiastical History*, ed. A. C. Zenos, *NPNF* 2.2.

Sozomen, *Ecclesiastical History*, ed. Chester D. Hartranft, *NPNF* 2.2.

Stories, Sermons, and Prayers of St. Nephon: An Ascetic Bishop, trans. Jeannie E. Gentithes and Ignatios Apostolopoulos (Minneapolis: Light and Life, 1989).

Symeon d-Taibutha, *The Book of Grace* (selections), trans. Dana R. Miller, in Isaac the Syrian, *Ascetical Homilies* (Boston: Holy Transfiguration Monastery, 1984), Appendix B.I.

Tertullian, *Against Marcion*, trans. Peter Holmes, *ANF* 3.

———, *The Crown* [or *The Chaplet*], trans. S. Thelwall, *ANF* 3.

———, *The Shows*, trans. S. Thelwall, *ANF* 3.

Theodoret of Cyrus, *The First Letter to the Corinthians*, trans. Robert Charles Hill, in *Commentary on the Letters of St. Paul* (Brookline: Holy Cross Orthodox Press, 2001).

The Virtues of Saint Macarius, trans. Tim Vivian, *PPS* 28.

The Author

Joel J. Miller has worked as a writer an editor for more than a decade. As the author of three previous books, including *The Revolutionary Paul Revere*, his work has been acclaimed as "lively" (*World*), "vibrant" (William J. Bennett), "well-researched and bitingly written" (*Publishers Weekly*), and "powerful" (*The Washington Times*). Joel's articles have been featured in *Reason*, *The American Spectator*, *National Review*, *RealClearReligion*, and other outlets. He blogs about faith and spirituality at JoelJMiller.com.

Joel and his wife Megan have four children and live in Nashville, Tennessee. You can contact him at JoelJMiller.com or via Twitter: @JoelJMiller.

Index

INDEX